CW01642600

Better

'Thought leaders are invited to embark on a journey of authentic growth and discovery with *Better* by Christina Wedgwood. This wonderful book challenges traditional notions of dominant thought leadership, inviting you to embrace authenticity and engage in open, honest, and mutually reinforcing conversations with followers and other leaders. Prepare to be moved, inspired, and empowered to take the first steps in sharing your unique perspective with the world.'

– Thomas Curran, professor of psychology at the London School of Economics and author of *The Perfection Trap*

'To the quiet, the considered, the ethical, the evidence-based, the kind – now, more than ever, the world needs to hear your great ideas. Struggling to take the first step? Read this wonderful book and let Christina's gentle wisdom guide and inspire you into action.'

– Russell Pickering, speaker, trainer, comms expert and author of *Step Into The Spotlight*

'Christina Wedgwood's new book *Better* is a testament to her extensive experience and deep understanding of what makes genuine leadership shine through and unite a team. With a rich background in empowering individuals to express their authenticity, Christina's practical guidance is invaluable to anyone seeking to lead with purpose and make a meaningful difference to our world.'

– Wendy Thompson, marketer, entrepreneur and founder of Thompson Spencer

'Christina has helped so many authors, so it's no surprise that *Better* is a winner. Christina makes us rethink everything we thought we knew about thought leadership, and helps us reimagine not only what it truly is, but shows how all of us can (and should) bring our unique ideas and perspective to the world. Can't recommend highly enough!'

– Suzi McAlpine, executive and leadership coach and author of *Beyond Burnout*

'This will be a valuable resource to those who know they can make a positive difference but have always considered that to be the domain of the natural extroverts. I know that this book will expand the diversity of voices for the greater good, and I encourage anyone who is curious about whether they could be one of those voices, to read this deep sharing from Christina. Like all things she does, it is well researched, deeply considered and content rich. Go buy it now!'

– Marisa Fong, entrepreneur, investor and mentor of women leaders

'If you want to have an impact in this world, but feel like you don't fit the mould of the 'influential thought leader', this book is for you. Far from being a highly-prescriptive, "twenty-seven and a half steps you must follow in this exact order" template, it is an invitation to reflect, play, and bring your special brand of magic to the world in your perfectly unique and authentic way. Because what the world needs right now is you showing up as YOU – and *Better* will help you do just that.'

– Daria Williamson, strengths coach and author of *Unleash Your Awesome*

'Christina's beautiful book challenges the narrow definitions of thought leadership, and shares why it is so critical for the future success of humanity to broaden these parameters, as well as sharing ideas for how each of us can step into our own unique magic to make the world better. Thank you for encouraging more inclusivity and diversity.'

– Dr Ellen Joan Ford, leadership speaker, facilitator
and author of *#WorkSchoolHours*

'If you're tired of the same old advice on thought leadership, this book is for you. Christina offers a new, more inclusive, and authentic approach that will resonate with anyone who wants to make a difference through their ideas, but doesn't feel they fit the mould of a typical thought leader.'

– Mark Hayes, Head of Growth Marketing at TASK Group

'So many of us are shoved around by a harsh Inner Critic that says we've got nothing valuable to say. We get hooked by the belief that our ideas don't matter, or that we must be a certain type of person to share them confidently. Meanwhile, the world is missing out on the unique gold we have to offer. *Better* shows us exactly how to cut through the Inner Critic's noise and recognise that our voice matters. Christina's expertise will enable you to walk a thought leadership path that works for you. Reading this book is so important. Because life is short. There's no time to waste holding back or playing small. The world is waiting to hear from you.'

– Dr Bex Bell, speaker, coach
and author of *Inner Critic to Inner Coach*

'To all the non-alpha people who want to have a voice—you have finally been heard! Christina sees you, sees us. She sees our value, our potential. Her book gives us a way to lead from where we are, no personality transplants required! You can do the work that matters most to you in a way that fits who you are.'

— Gillian Brookes, fexible work specialist and author of *Flexperts*

'Christina Wedgwood empowers readers to embrace their unique strengths and make a difference on their own terms. With a blend of empathy and expertise, she guides readers through the process of overcoming reluctance and embracing authenticity in their leadership journey. Whether you're a seasoned expert or just starting out, this book provides invaluable guidance for anyone looking to increase their impact and contribute to a better world.'

— Denise Brosseau, author of *Ready to Be a Thought Leader?*

'Better breaks down the artificial walls of a crowded and noisy space, and creates room for those reluctant to share their ideas for fear of not fitting in. In this book Christina delivers a masterclass and shows us a different way to make an impact through fresh ideas in a world starving for real and authentic thought leadership.'

— Konstantinos Apostolopoulos, bestselling author of *The Engagement Blueprint*

Better

A more authentic path for the reluctant thought leader

Christina Wedgwood

INTELLIGENT INK PRESS
CLEVER THINGS WITH WORDS

INTELLIGENT INK PRESS
CLEVER THINGS WITH WORDS

Published by Intelligent Ink Press

© Christina Wedgwood 2024
The moral right of the author has been asserted

Typeset by YourBooks
Cover design by Hannah Boom

Produced by Intelligent Ink Press
www.intelligentink.co.nz

All rights reserved. Without limiting the rights under copyright above, no part of this publication may be reproduced, stored in a retrieval system, or transmitted, in any format or by any means (electronic, mechanical, photocopying, recording or otherwise), without the prior written permission of both the copyright owner and the publisher of this book.

A catalogue record for this book is available from the National Library of New Zealand.

ISBN 978-1-7386201-6-6

For the quiet ones

CONTENTS

Introduction

Everyone who has great ideas, and who is doing great work, should be able to have the impact that they want to have in the world. We'd all be better off with more creative, innovative, inclusive and beneficial ideas out there.

Absolutely you can volunteer or advocate; you could start a business, charity or social enterprise. Those are all important and worthwhile vehicles for change. But what if you could also, or instead, achieve positive impact through sharing your ideas and thinking, through showing a different and better way forward, through driving others to take positive action? What if there was a uniquely "you" way of showing up and amplifying the magic of what you do?

Thought leadership is a vehicle for all of this – but, for the most part, we have far too narrow a definition of what thought leadership is and far too small a box for who gets to be one.

This is what we are here to change, so that it's possible for all of us to bring our unique brand of magic to the world. So that there's more space for those who care – and who genuinely want to contribute based on what they know and what they do – to make an impact.

This might feel and sound very different to what you already know about thought leadership: that it's some sacred position bestowed on those who can rouse thousands through their performance up on stage, or captivate millions via a podcast. That it goes hand-in-hand with lucrative book deals whose titles quickly make their way to the top of the bestseller lists. That it requires saturation of particular ideas until they become part of our day-to-day vocabulary.

But what about those of us who aren't ex-marketing professionals, or graduates of the Big Three, and who aren't sporting CVs that feature several Fortune 500 companies? What about those of us who don't always sound slick and polished, or who don't necessarily *want* to take up masses of space, or act big, bold and brash in sharing what we're doing? Just as we have come to understand that a leader isn't only someone with a job title or positional power within their organisational chart, a thought leader isn't only the loudest foghorn in the cacophony of noise.

While these dominant ideas of thought leadership have no doubt spelt success for a select few, those same ideas have also excluded the quieter, more thoughtful, or more reserved among us – those who have the potential to bring better thinking to the world but have largely, until now, equated influence with "ick".

If you want to help more people and see meaningful change in the world through your ideas, but don't want to force yourself into a narrow archetype, then this book is for you. Together, we will explore an alternative path as we celebrate the power in recognising and valuing different ideas, personalities, and ways of showing up beyond the larger-than-life personas that we have historically revered.

We all want some aspect or element to be improved by the fact that we are here. We want the fact that we know some things and did some things – that we took some chances, figured stuff out, and tried – to matter. Yet too many people don't get to see their great work achieve the impact it could, and it's almost exclusively because of the pernicious idea that thought leadership belongs to a certain type of person.

We need more ideas and solutions out there. And we need *your* ideas and solutions out there. We are living in volatile and complex times, and facing an uncertain and precarious future. With more and more intersections of technology and humanity, there are exponentially more places for both change and chaos to emerge.[1] But this means that there are also more places where opportunity and ingenuity are possible – if we can broaden out the boundaries and loosen up, or expand on, the so-called "rules".

The same thinking that's created or allowed these problems to exist is not what we need more of if we hope to solve them. If we keep listening only to the same people – those with positional power, those consistently speaking the loudest, and those more focused on status than real change – then we risk continuing to marginalise and alienate the clever people and great ideas that are waiting patiently in the background. If instead we look more widely, and listen more carefully, we will discover new perspectives and insights from those who haven't spoken up yet, or often. They're going to come from people like you. We need to hear from more of the watchers, the thinkers, and the reflectors who take their time in formulating their ideas. And that's not only because I am one. It's also because it is only through an inclusive effort towards better thinking that we can tap into the full potential of our collective creativity and problem-solving power. This is how we're going to best ensure the wellbeing of our world.

Imagine a world where everyone is empowered to speak up, and all great ideas were celebrated and heard. We would form a chorus of ideas to tackle problems from different angles. We'd create spaces where creativity, innovation and a collaborative propensity towards problem-solving were welcomed. We'd create a world where active, informed and respectful debate could flourish, helping us to appreciate that the world has never been "simply" one thing or another.

This type of discourse is not frequently seen, but it's what we need. Research has found that when we think together, as well as when we argue (in the right way), we experience deeper learning, arrive at sounder decisions, and develop more innovative solutions.[2] I personally don't love arguing, but some conflict is unavoidable, and there is something to be said for productive debate. 'Honest disagreement,' as Mahatma Gandhi is believed to have said, 'is often a good sign of progress.'[3] So, if that is the process by which we will move forward, then we need to get more voices involved. We need to bring more viewpoints to the table in a way that welcomes productive discussion.

Right now, we're playing in too small a space. Too many of us have taken to heart the idea that "You must be *this tall* to ride". Those who feel they don't fit the paradigm are turning away (or getting turned away) from exploring the potential of thought leadership. However, different approaches can be far more advantageous and effective than the current model would have us think. There's nothing wrong with loud and outgoing – but those people are likely to sound out their perspectives regardless. I want to invite and encourage the ones who otherwise might not be heard.

It's time we shift the borders and move the edges out – not just lifting up the tent flaps, but tearing down the walls so that anyone can step in. It's time we celebrate and welcome alternative paths that are not only valid, but valuable.

In this book, you will not find a prescriptive process to achieve impact with your ideas. Given that a central tenet here is that there is no one "right" way to influence with your ideas, trying to then provide a best path would be hypocritical. Instead, we are going to broaden out our understanding of what it means to build thought leadership, why you would want to, and what it can look like. We're going to look at four pillars you can lean into, in our own authentic way, to achieve better thinking, better outcomes and better impact and influence. We're going to shift our perspectives and dip our toes in. Think of it as an exploration rather than an explanation, and a launching off rather than a landing point. Just as our individual impacts will be varied, surprising, uplifting and uniquely magical, let's allow our paths to getting there to be similarly so. There's room for all of us, but we need to do things differently.

My hope is that this book will fan the flames for those who have a spark but may still be diminishing it. In *You Are a Badass,* Jen Sincero urges us all to surround ourselves with 'people who act on their big ideas, who take action on making positive change in the world and who see nothing as out of their reach'. I'm lucky enough to know many of these people and I'm here to champion you to not only find your own people like this, but to be one of those people, too.

Solving big problems requires not only our sustained focus, but also our ability to rethink and remain flexible about what we believe we know. Works like *Stolen Focus* by Johann Hari and *Think Again* by Adam Grant present the urgency of improving our capacity for thinking. Tara Mohr speaks largely to women in *Playing Big*, similarly urging women's greater participation to make our world better, while imploring them to turn away from narrow labels that stop them from fulfilling their potential. *Quiet* by Susan Cain and *The Introvert's Edge* by Matthew Pollard have made excellent headway into widening our ideas of success beyond that of the assertive, bold and confident archetype, too. These books all provide valuable tips and tools, but they stop short of showing us where to practically channel our efforts towards change. To me, thought leadership is still an important and effective vehicle for having an out-sized impact.

Much attention has already been given to the how-to of thought leadership, with plenty of advice to help you design business models and leverageable assets. Aspiring thought leaders have plenty of resources on processes and principles to follow, especially around the ability to build and market their brand. Matt Church's *The Thought Leaders Practice* and Denise Brosseau's *Ready to be a Thought Leader?* are useful for this kind of help, though there is very little page count dedicated to the internal change needed to become a thought leader, or to the ways that we can broaden the field to make room for more voices. For this reason, my research builds on the above works to consider how we can apply authenticity to a space not necessarily known for its gentleness, and show up as we are to achieve success. I want you to imagine a new, more inclusive way forward to better thinking, better outcomes, and better impact or influence, without having to remake yourself. I am absolutely convinced that the qualities or aspects that so many of us think exclude us from thought leadership can be our superpowers.

I started Intelligent Ink in April 2011, motivated to help people and businesses who were doing cool things but not communicating those things very well. Some were trying to tell the world what they were about via their websites, magazine columns, or various other pieces of content, but they needed help lifting their message with sharper writing. There were commercial clients who were doing incredible things but undermining themselves or selling themselves short, and not-for-profits who had incredible success stories that, to them, were ordinary Tuesdays not worth making a fuss over. I wanted our skills as an agency to help people to shine, get the credit and recognition they deserved, and inspire others.

While Intelligent Ink has changed quite a bit since then, those principles still apply. Today, we're proudly claiming a niche that sees us helping purpose-driven experts build thought leadership and have an incredible impact with their ideas. Whether they are coaches making a transformational difference in their clients' lives, consultants revolutionising the way organisations work, or businesses providing better solutions in their industries, every day we help people build their intellectual property, reputations and impact, and provide value to more people than would otherwise be possible based on their capacity and calendar. It's hugely rewarding work; I feel lucky to be in the privileged position of recognising how incredible these people are and how important the work they do is, and reflecting that back to them. It's no small thing that I've got to see work, words and positive ripples out in the world that would not have been there had it not been for what our team is doing. Together, we've made a difference.

That difference has not happened because we can provide comprehensive content calendars or workable posting schedules. Our combined impact is not the result of knowing secrets for hacking algorithms or having a prescribed process that we force everyone through. Instead, we've achieved what we have by listening to clever and caring people who are doing amazing work, and helping them unlock *their* expertise and confidence. Many of them do not fit the dominant mould for thought leadership, but, with our support and guidance, they can lean further into who they are, while amplifying what they're doing.

These are my people. But it's also true that these people are me. I deeply understand the resistance they experience, because much of it is what I have encountered, too. And what I still encounter. I share their concerns and distaste for the bravado and noise. When I think about venturing further than what I'm currently comfortable doing, I feel the same fears that I have helped them to face. I am a reluctant thought leader, but also someone who operates from a place of authenticity. I'm not trying to be Simon Sinek, Brené Brown, or even my much more outgoing colleague Verity Craft, and nor should I feel I have to be. But I will learn from and be inspired by their work and their ways of being, and take that with me as I evolve my own thought leadership position and the way I show up in the world. I'm on the same path as many of you: working to make something better and increase the impact of what we're doing, in a way that works with who we are.

•••

We'll be taking the journey from reluctant to authentic thought leader together throughout the course of this book. Part 1 starts with framing our current understanding of what constitutes thought leadership, dismantling our preconceptions and lowering the bar for entry into the field. In Chapter 1, we detail the familiar model of thought leadership or influence as it stands today: the archetype of the loud, confident and too-certain sage on the stage. This dominant persona isn't necessarily a new phenomenon, but the result of centuries of thinking around what makes a successful leader. Little wonder, then, that this archetype is alienating for those who want to have impact, but feel like they're swimming against the tide. So the chapter also raises the prospect of widening the pool.

Chapter 2 shows why leading with our ideas is increasingly necessary in a volatile and uncertain world, and why it matters that we improve the realm of thought leadership through our contributions. The result is that the definition of a successful thought leader starts to widen, and we begin to appreciate those examples that appear in more places than the front of an auditorium or saturating the internet. Resistance is the focus of Chapter 3. While it may appear that others don't experience worry, entering new territory or pushing towards something better means that you should expect some uncertainty. Here you will be reassured that your reluctance is normal, and can even be a good thing. Chapter 4 drills us down into the idea of authenticity. We know that slick marketing and displays of confidence are effective, but it is your authentic, self-aligned brand of thought leadership that will always win the day. This is not only more effective with those you are here for, but alignment is also vital in allowing you to show up sustainably every day and have a lasting impact. Before the end of Part 1, we will begin to form our vision for what better looks like and imagine a new, more inclusive, and broader version of thought leadership.

In Part 2, we explore four qualities needed for better. From embracing complexity and acknowledging uncertainty, to sharing our ideas in an inclusive and collaborative way, and always evolving and improving what we're doing, together these qualities form the antithesis of what we often get now. They bring the broadening and the balance that are so sorely needed in thought leadership.

We will see in Chapter 5 that, while simplification can be helpful, it can also go too far – especially when it comes to ideas. We risk losing some of the picture, and often some of the truth, when simple information is put forward as fact and the full story. Here we see the value of leaning into nuance to create better understanding and solutions, and to allow us to craft more compelling arguments. In Chapter 6, you will be reassured that you don't need to know everything. We will acknowledge that while communicating confidently and decisively makes it seem like we know what we're talking about, humbly acknowledging uncertainty can be equally powerful and can lead to better outcomes. In Chapter 7, we are reminded that encouraging and inspiring others is a key part of leadership, and we will see that when we present with less certainty and ask questions, we leave room for others – inspiring their thinking, engagement and buy-in. This chapter builds a further case that true impact comes from conversations, not from a one-way sermon delivered from literal or symbolic stages. Chapter 8 helps us overcome our "not ready yet" reluctance. Although you need to have value in your ideas and have your thinking in a place that makes it ready to share, it's also a good thing that you will continue learning, and change your mind as you grow. Allowing your thinking to develop and evolve – and including others on that journey – is a powerful way to build trust and encourage others' rethinking also.

Chapter 9 concludes the book by taking all of what we've considered and showing you how you can take action along an alternative and, for you, a more authentic path towards thought leadership.

It's not easy to gain influence, amplify your voice and increase your impact, and there is no one-size-fits-all approach, yet there is room for growth and celebration on our own terms. Successful thought leaders are those who have found a way to align the impact they want to have with their own personality and style; they're changing hearts and minds and delivering better outcomes in a way that works with who they are. In order to do this, they have given themselves permission to try, change and grow, and they are showing others what's possible. If I can make the small moves to start to overcome my resistance and stop hiding, you can, too. I don't want to see any one of us playing small or doubting our voice. So, in the ultimate act of putting myself out into the world, I've written this book – packed full of alternative perspectives, reframes and possibilities that I believe can help.

While this mission has been both personally and professionally pressing, it isn't just for me – nor is it even just for the other reluctant thought leaders who might read it.

It's for all of us.

Part One

CHAPTER 1

Expanding the circle

It's Saturday morning. You're up and dressed – and not in your usual weekend wardrobe of activewear either. You're in work mode. You have your notebook out and ready in your lap, a takeaway coffee in hand, and you're packed alongside more than a thousand other people into the conference centre. You have only a vague idea of what the day has in store for you, and you're not quite sure how you got talked into being here over the weekend. You're thinking about the slow start and pancakes you'd much rather have had, and what the rest of your family will be doing this morning instead, especially given the sun is shining. You're here now, though; you figure you might as well embrace it. Heck, you might even learn something!

The overhead lights dim and a hush spreads across the crowd. Those in the audience around you shuffle in their seats. Phones and the last dregs of coffee disappear. Pens and notebooks are picked up in readiness.

There's a moment of breath before upbeat music blares out of the speakers, and a spotlight swings from the back of the room to focus on the front of the stage. Out bounds Jack. He's 30- or 40-something, dressed in an accessibly expensive button-down and designer jeans, hair gelled and coiffed to perfection. He's just about skipping. Even before he's opened his mouth, you can sense his mega-watt energy and enthusiasm for being up there; he's excited about what he's here to share, and that attitude is infectious. Maybe this isn't such a bad way to spend your Saturday, after all. You feel your spirits lift, hopeful that you'll get some value from being here.

The music fades and Jack launches in and begins his presentation. Despite being mic'd, he's practically yelling. His accent belies that he's well-travelled. Amid carefully choreographed hand gestures, he projects that he's sure of both himself and what he's up there to say. As well he should be. Jack's an award-winning entrepreneur, bestselling author, TV host, podcaster, high-profile investor, a regular on the lists of the young and rich, and he's flown in to spread his message further and recruit Kiwi followers. With his big, bold persona and impressive rap sheet of external validation, we're well used to sitting up and paying attention to this particular brand of thought leadership.

•••

Jack may be special, but he's not unique. Not on the surface, at least. Jack's our archetypal thought leader and, chances are, you can call to mind any number of 'Jacks' you've seen both off and on the stage. We've all come across, and been influenced by, these characters. It's hard to escape them, prominent as they are. You will have seen them on social media, been forwarded and linked to their articles, listened to their interviews, or stumbled across their podcast pages. Their profiles are prolific – it seems like they're everywhere.

And when you do encounter them? They're a bold personality owning the stage, like a rock star or mega-church pastor who has won over massive audiences and, we assume, also boasts a long line of book deals and big cheques thanks to their vast network of effortless business connections. They ooze charisma and spout sharp and sexy soundbites, delivering their message in a way that's polished, practised and persuasive. And while they're talking a big game and being excited about the idea (or thing) they're selling, it can be hard, at times, to see whether there's substance behind their impressive show.

Jack is the archetype of a thought leader today: the sage on the stage. This term originates from the field of education, and was used to describe the traditional teaching method whereby a central figure in the classroom – the teacher or professor – imparts their knowledge by lecturing to the class. It's a useful description for thought leadership, too. After all, our understanding of what a stage is has grown beyond classrooms, auditoriums, theatres and stadiums, and now includes social platforms, blogs, YouTube channels and podcasts. Our stages now increasingly include digital spaces, where connecting with thousands of people can be achieved with just a few clicks. And there are people prepared to use these spaces to share their message and convert followers to their big ideas.

Whether in the physical or digital realm (or both), what

we're talking about when we think of the sage on the stage is the stream of seemingly endless and one-way information shared from a public platform to an audience. The individual activities they are engaged in matter far, far less than the collection of traits that we bestow upon these people. We perceive them to be confident, commanding and performative, with fully-formed and highly polished ideas ready to dazzle us with. As a result, the sage on the stage rules supreme. Yet it's a near unattainable standard to reach. That's what needs to change.

It makes sense that we've arrived here

It doesn't take big leaps of imagination to see how we arrived at this dominant archetype. Just a couple of decades ago, an expert was simply someone who knew more about a subject than most people, and their input was valued and sought out. The rise of the internet – with both its noble intentions and more challenging products – brought to our fingertips more information than we could possibly need. It levelled the playing field, and suddenly anyone could effectively, ostensibly, be an expert.

Knowing things became no longer enough when anyone could do that. Now people needed to become *known* for knowing things. Great thinking was increasingly only part of the equation; the leadership aspect was demanded more and more. Those who really wanted to have an impact needed to be able to take ideas and knowledge and inspire people to act upon that information, creating impact while building a reputation around their ability to influence. It's only natural, then, that our great thinkers – those with good ideas or who were doing great work – would look to those who have historically had the ability to persuade or mobilise the masses. And so the qualities and expectations of great leadership began to encroach on the realm of the expert.

The tactics and traits that comprise our idea of what leadership looks like and requires have filtered down from politicians and public speakers to business owners and entrepreneurs, and through to those within organisations who have worked to find and use their voices. Whether these people's ideas were what endowed them with their position of power, or whether their powerful positions meant their words were then bestowed with more weight, we have nevertheless seen aspiring thought leaders adopt and borrow many traits of the people we perceive to be effective leaders. From carrying themselves with confidence, speaking boldly and with conviction, acting with authority, and asserting certainties that leave very little room for argument, our model of a successful thought leader owes more to what we considered to be effective leadership than effective thinking. Mix in a bit of marketing and communications (vital for the "being known for knowing things" part), and we've got the culturally-created combination of what we think thought leadership ought to be.

This has only been reinforced by our cognitive bias towards displays of confidence that sees us so easily convinced by those who seem sure of things. Despite the firm hold this mental model has on us, there is actually very little real overlap between confidence and competence. In her hugely influential book *Quiet: The Power of Introverts in a World That Can't Stop Talking,* Susan Cain shares research in group dynamics that backs up the often-felt but rarely-said-out-loud tendency to perceive talkers as being smarter than quieter types.[4] I have seen this already in action with my chatty and precocious youngest son who has, on more than one occasion and by more than one person, been the subject of speculation that he might be "gifted". Only time will reveal whether this is the case (or whether it even really matters one way or another), but it's an effective example of how we make judgements about people based on what they put out into the world by way of talking – even when we don't have any experience of their internal world, nor know how busy or rich that may be.

Not only do we typically see those who are talking as smarter than others, Cain also points out that fast talkers are considered more competent and likeable than those who speak more slowly. They seem more certain, and that means we tend to believe what they are saying. We are more likely to see someone who is doing more of the talking as the leader, too. Organisational psychologist and author of *Hidden Potential,* Adam Grant refers to this as the "babble effect", and points to research showing that groups will promote the people who command the most airtime. It makes sense in some ways, because the more a person talks, the more we direct our attention towards them, and the increasingly powerful that person appears to become as a result. But the trouble is this: 'We get stuck following people who dominate the discussion instead of those who elevate it.'[5]

This wouldn't be so bad if more talking was correlated with greater insights, but research suggests that this is not the case.[6] Just as being in a position of power doesn't necessarily make you an effective leader, talking more (or more loudly) doesn't automatically make someone's ideas any more valuable, or right. My son might be showing us more of the machinations of his mind with his near-constant verbal expression, but that doesn't mean his thought quality is any higher or necessarily more insightful than that of his quieter peers. Again, time will tell.

Our tendency to equate talking with smarts persists even in the face of evidence across grade-point averages, SATs, and IQ test scores that reveal very little difference between quiet and louder people in those measures of intelligence.[7] While on some level we can all understand that there is zero correlation between the gift of the gab and good ideas, we nevertheless all (and often) fall prey to our bias towards displays of confidence, or get caught in the grips of great showmanship. Charismatic and enchanting people excel at selling a vision, providing meaning, and giving people hope. Yet when those same people are incompetent, lack purpose or are not well-meaning, the power of their charisma means they may come across well but completely fail to back it up with any benefits. Putting on a good show distracts us, for a while at least, from the fact that we've been had. And the consequences can be far-reaching. Psychologists have noted that people will be more likely to tolerate a bad president who is charismatic than they would tolerate a high-performing president who is not.[8]

It turns out that it's not wholly our fault, but rather the result of programming that takes root from our youngest years. Despite there being scant evidence that higher confidence correlates to better leadership or better thinking, the perception is planted early. When Cain interviewed primary-school teachers about the shift towards more cooperative or group learning, she received this comment from a teacher of children around nine or 10 years old: 'This style of teaching reflects the business community, where people's respect for each other is based on their verbal abilities, not their originality or insight. You have to be someone who speaks well and calls attention to yourself. It's an elitism based on something other than merit.'[9] In other words, from a young age, we're surrounded by evidence that sounding good and asserting yourself confidently seems to be what wins the day. That idea takes root and sets us up with expectations of effectiveness as we go through school and, later, enter the workforce. My youngest son is already being praised for his "sparkle", yet I see some incredibly profound thoughts and interesting observations come from my middle son who, perhaps because of a speech delay and challenges around pronunciation, asserted himself much less, especially in his younger years.

We're doing our best to lessen the influence of these biases in our home. But all of this comes about because we live firmly in the grip of the "extroverted ideal" – a values system based around the belief that the ideal self is gregarious, alpha and comfortable in the spotlight. As Cain explains, this ideal prizes action over contemplation, risk-taking over heed-taking, and certainty over doubt. 'We're told that to be great is to be bold, to be happy is to be sociable,' she writes.[10] Or to be sparkly and chatty is to be lovable, interesting, and potentially gifted in my son's case. These stories are both deeply held and powerful, and they reflect what is most rewarded.

In *The Introvert's Edge: How the Quiet and Shy Can Outsell Anyone*, author Matthew Pollard reinforces Cain's views, similarly explaining that we live in a world (at least, in Eurocentric countries) that looks up to people who act like extroverts. We describe the leaders we admire as "outgoing", "charming" and "charismatic", and in so doing internalise the belief that successful people look and act this way. The research reinforces this: Adam Grant, Francesca Gino and David A. Hofmann's work looking at the relationship between personality and leadership found that extroversion was the most consistently correlated trait with leadership, leading to something they called the "extroverted leadership advantage".

As one of my favourite gregarious extroverts – my colleague Verity Craft – admitted to me, having those attributes doesn't make her any smarter, nor does it mean that she has better ideas. In fact, she concedes that the opposite is often true. However, these traditionally prized attributes undoubtedly have made her life easier; they are a form of privilege. 'People tend to listen to me and I'm generally better able to do the things I want,' Verity shared in a discussion about the benefits of extroversion. Luckily, Verity has cultivated enough humility and self-awareness not to take advantage of that, but the fact remains that these traits are positively reinforced by others, as well as in experiences of being effective in the world. This is how we end up with our beliefs about the people we should model, and the behaviours we should value and strive for.

There are other factors at play, too. Amid increasing social, organisational and technological complexity, we increasingly want straight-forward answers. While simple and certain-seeming solutions have always been attractive, they've taken on an even greater allure in our busier-than-ever lives. "Sure things" have become more marketable; they're easier to sell to the uncertain, the confused, the overwhelmed. And who doesn't feel at least a little that way nowadays? Add to that the fact that we've had an explosion of communication channels over which to broadcast our thinking, and you get double the impact. We're overloaded, with more options than we could ever possibly hope to attend to, so we're constantly having to choose how we navigate the bombardment.

When faced with audiences that are making snap judgements about what they will give their attention to, there is a tendency to serve up only the ideas that look or sound good immediately, or perhaps those that address one part of a situation while ignoring the others. Again, confidence and simplicity often get a bigger share of our attention than nuance or complexity does. We've come to favour what can be broadcast easily – and the ideas that have the most promise of travelling are those that have been stripped down into sexy soundbites.

The result of all this is that we've had a generation of leaders and thinkers who are scrambling to control the narrative, with all of them trying to yell the loudest as they compete to be heard. In too many cases, we've conflated volume for accuracy and worth. And we've ended up with a whole lot of what I call the "three Bs": bluster, bravado and bullshit. Unfortunately, all of this has also shaped a pervasive idea of what thought leadership takes, what it looks like, and who deserves to be talking – and it's an unsavoury image that is putting many of the smartest people off contributing to the world with their ideas.

The damage being done

If we safely assume that most people – whether they are the quiet or the talkative types – have roughly the same number of good ideas, then it's a problem if only the louder and more forceful people are sharing theirs. As Cain asserts: 'This would mean that an awful lot of bad ideas prevail while good ones get squashed.'[11] Or, I'd add, are never heard in the first place. Frankly, we can't afford that. We need to challenge the dominant ideas of who should be talking. Our society is facing numerous challenges, from pandemics to climate change, cultural tensions, mental health crises, divisiveness, inequality, and injustices. This list isn't showing signs of shrinking (yet), and it's more than we should be prepared to accept. We have a pressing need for innovation, and that means we need all the great ideas that we can get.

But just having great ideas isn't enough on its own. We need to make our ideas available, so that others can benefit from them. That's why I see thought leadership as an important vehicle, and the starting point for all progress and innovation. It couples the development of ideas with the inspiring of action in a way that helps us all to move towards better outcomes, better solutions, and a better future. And with the future at stake, it's of urgent importance that we are hearing from everyone who has something of value to contribute.

To be clear, there's nothing inherently wrong with being outgoing or confident; just like their opposites, these traits have both their benefits and their blind spots. Nor is there anything wrong with a simple and spiffy soundbite that gets cut-through (so long as it is backed up by robust thinking). If we continue down the road of one type of thought leader, however, we're inevitably going to get more of one type of thinking. Not only do we need far more diversity than that, but we also need our collective ideascape to be more inclusive. If we celebrate, revere and respond to only one type of thought leader, then we will continue to miss out on the voices and ideas of those who don't feel as though they fit the mould. We need to hear from everyone who is engaging in great work, not just those who are used to talking. If we don't allow for dissenting views, there can be disastrous consequences.

In *Quiet*, Cain shares a story about the 2008 financial crash that serves as a cautionary tale for what happens when only one type of person so totally controls the narrative. Since that time there has been plenty of speculation about whether we'd have been better off with more women (or less testosterone) on Wall Street. Taking this idea further, Cain poses the question of what might have happened if we'd had more introverts at the helm – in other words, what would have happened if we'd had different types of thinkers making the decisions?

Her question is answered, at least in part, by Boykin Curry, a managing director of the investment firm Eagle Capital, who had front-row seats to the 2008 financial meltdown. To his mind, too much power (and therefore too much of the dominant voice that was being listened to) was concentrated in the hands of aggressive risk-takers. Just like the cultural conditioning that has understandably led to us being where we are in terms of thought leadership, it was a slow yet slippery slope that enabled this situation to take root as well. As Curry explains,

> For twenty years, the DNA of nearly every financial institution [...] morphed dangerously. Each time someone at the table pressed for more leverage and more risk, the next few years proved them 'right'. Those people were emboldened, they were promoted and they gained control of ever more capital. Meanwhile, anyone in power who hesitated, who argued for caution, was

> proved 'wrong'. The cautious types were increasingly intimidated, passed over for promotion. They lost their hold on capital. This happened almost every day in almost every financial institution, over and over, until we ended up with a very specific type of person running things.[12]

Not only did many fail to understand the risks the banks were taking, but those who did were consistently ignored. To Curry's mind, it was forceful extroverts who caused the global financial crash: 'People with certain personality types got control of capital and institutions and power – and people who were congenitally more cautious and introverted and statistical in their thinking became discredited and pushed aside.'[13]

Contrast this with one of the best-known introverted leaders: Mark Zuckerberg. In the same period as the lead-up to the financial crash, Facebook (now Meta, with Facebook and Instagram among its services) was still in its start-up stages, and hitting its first 100 million users. That may seem plenty, but is a far cry from the 3-billion-plus monthly active users that the platform has at the time of writing.[14] Despite Zuckerberg succeeding in securing investment, there were concerns that a social network couldn't be monetised the same way that search-engines – a proven business model by this stage – had been. Zuckerberg still needed to figure out the optimum model and create solid revenue streams to account for their high valuation.

Like all businesses at that time, Facebook had to weather the global financial storm. However, they followed a flexible and considered approach. Instead of a big and bold play, the company went back to basics: thinking more carefully about what their core business was and looking at the core service they were providing – advertising – then adapting that to the situation that the world was in.[15] Facebook not only weathered the storm, but they came out of the global financial crisis stronger: in September 2009 the company reported being cashflow-positive for the first time.[16] These may seem like extreme examples, and it's possible not to love all of the things these organisations represent, but they help us to see the facts: we need more types of thinking to be heard, and more ways of being to be valued.

Introverts are not smarter than extroverts, however, they do think differently. Extroverts often excel at tasks involving multitasking, information overload, and those performed under time or social pressure. Introverts, meanwhile, tend to think more carefully; they're more reflective, taking time to digest information thoroughly and consider more varied inputs. They also tend to stay on-task longer and work more accurately. As Cain explains, extroverts focus more on what's happening here and now (the "What is … ?" questions), while introverts recall events from the past and make plans for the future with wonder and imagination (the "What if … ?" questions).

I understand that it's not simply the case that those thought leaders who fit the dominant archetype are extroverted, or that all the introverts are currently scared into silence. That dichotomy would be too simplistic. I've seen people from varied places on the introvert–extrovert continuum experience reluctance about thought leadership. The important point is that we still have a problematic divide between those who feel capable of fitting the type and those who see thought leadership as an avenue available only to others.

When all the airtime is being taken up by those who are used to talking, there's very little room left for others to find their voices. As Cain asserts: 'Our reverence for alpha status blinds us to things that are good and smart and wise.'[17] I see so many great thinkers and clever, generous changemakers who are scared into staying small. They're influenced by the current model of what someone succeeding in the thought leadership sphere looks like, and because they don't see themselves that way, they write it off as an avenue that they could pursue. They don't see that they could have space to play, so they hold back their contributions. They simply cannot see a way that they would be prepared to fit.

Many of them are engaged in doing incredible work and are making a significant impact within their network and client base. Yet they have an idea of what a thought leader should be like, and, because they don't identify with that image, they believe the label could never belong to them. They stick to doing what they do within their own circle, closed to the possibility of making a greater impact or leading with their ideas. When that is the case, the rest of us are missing out.

There's another reason we need more varied people in the mix, too: diverse groups are better than homogenous expert groups at finding solutions to specific challenges. Studies have shown that drawing on diversity means that, rather than just building a more complete picture of an issue, we also ensure we create a more accurate one.[18] We tend to think of diversity along the lines of inbuilt traits like age, gender identity, ethnicity, race, and sexual orientation; however, there are other differences that are equally important. Decision -making and appreciation of the bigger picture are significantly aided by diversity in personality, temperament, and thinking or processing styles, too. In virtually any sphere, we're better off if we bring together people with varied strengths, experiences, industry backgrounds, and areas of study or specialty.

When a diverse group approaches solving a problem, they bring different information, opinions, experiences and perspectives. Where we have openness and a shared purpose, we are provoked to think better and differently by hearing dissenting views from someone who we perceive as different.

In describing her research for *Scientific American*, Columbia Business School Professor Katherine Phillips details an experiment to examine the impact of racial diversity on small decision-making groups.[19] In this experiment, like in so much of our lives, sharing information was a requirement for success. What she found was that the groups of similar racial identity erroneously assumed that they all held the same information and shared the same perspective.This stopped them from effectively sharing and processing the information they had available to perform the task at hand, and it hindered creativity and innovation.

Where people were more obviously and overtly different to others in their group, they slowed down and engaged differently – ultimately outperforming the groups with no racial diversity. Phillips concluded that diversity 'encourages the search for novel information and perspectives, leading to better decision-making and problem-solving'. In other words, simply being exposed to diversity changes (and improves) the way we think.

The power of diversity, then, is far more than a statistical representation, but encompasses the contributions of each person. And it pays. When all voices contribute, the results are greater innovation and productivity and, for businesses, higher revenue.[20] Organisations that welcome diverse voices and perspectives are more productive and profitable, have more engaged teams, and are more flexible and resilient. Businesses are waking up to the fact that they need to make sure that all people are heard. From sending questions prior to the meeting to allow for more forethought, to establishing rules that encourage full participation, and facilitating meetings in a way that ensures that everyone can contribute (and that it's not just the same outgoing people dominating the agenda), there's much more conscious focus and proactive effort – by good leaders, at least – to ensure inclusion and to gather diverse thoughts.

This isn't only important in the boardroom or on Wall Street, though; it's important in the world. Thought leader and author Greg McKeown said that: 'In the cacophony of voices, it's often the quiet ones that hold the answers.'[21] I don't know if that is always true, but I would bet that it often is. So, we need all the people with great ideas, and on-their-way-to-great ideas, adding their input. One size very rarely fits all, so let's broaden the boundaries to create more space for other types to be effective. Only when everyone is given the tools and encouragement they need to share their considered viewpoints, varied perspectives and rich experiences, can we move forward with the best ideas and solutions.

Right now, we risk continuing to hold too tightly onto our dominant model of thought leadership and so continue to put too many people off. We will all be better off when we have a variety of viewpoints in our collective ideascape, and in the conversations shaped by thought leadership – especially if we hope to arrive at inclusive solutions that consider, and work for, all people.

So far:

We know that we have a dominant image of thought leadership, and we can absolutely see how this has come to have the stronghold it does.

Current thinking about thought leadership appears to prize:

- big, bold, confident personalities
- slick and polished presentations by confident, experienced speakers
- simple and stripped-down (sometimes to the point of being vacuous) soundbites
- assertions made with unwavering certainty
- opinions stated as authoritative facts, and
- information that functions as the final word.

Obviously not all examples of thought leadership look entirely this way, but you'd be forgiven for creating a picture that comprises these elements. And for being put off by it. This narrow picture of thought leadership is causing too many great thinkers and clever operators to stay quiet – and means we're missing out on so many great ideas that we would otherwise have access to.

CHAPTER 2

Unique perspectives and the ideascape

As a young girl growing up in Vienna in the 1920s, Hedwig used to go on walks around the 19th District with her father, Emil. They were both interested in technology, so as they walked Emil would explain to Hedwig the way that the things they encountered worked. From the street cars to the electric trolleys and the factories generating power, Hedwig learnt to associate invention with the father that she adored.

From the age of five, Hedwig had been interested in gadgets, taking apart her music-box and putting it back together again in order to see how it worked. And at the private school she attended, chemistry class was by far Hedwig's favourite part of the day because she got to 'mix things'.[22] As Hedwig grew older, that love for tinkering and experimentation remained. She worked a demanding day job – clocking long hours, six days a week – but after work, instead of going to bed or going out socialising, Hedwig was inventing. She had a worktable set up in her home to support her hobby. Hedwig didn't even feel like she had to work hard for ideas; they came naturally to her.

In 1940, war was ravaging Europe. Hedwig was, by that stage, living in the then-neutral United States. She had left her Jewish background far behind her, yet much of her heart remained in the place she had once called home. Hedwig was haunted by worry, fearing for her mother who had just fled Austria for London and was preparing to cross the Atlantic. Hedwig would stay up late into the night, listening to the latest news on the radio.

That summer, Hedwig heard about a ship that had been hit by a torpedo, killing everyone on board, including 83 children. Hedwig's fire was lit; she couldn't sit idly by. She resolved to do something that would even the balance for the British at sea. She believed a radio-controlled torpedo might do just that. The challenge, at that time at least, was that you could not secure radio communications. So Hedwig came up with a way of guiding a torpedo to a target with a signal that couldn't be interrupted or jammed, an idea she referred to as "frequency hopping". She thought it could work, but she didn't know how to make it happen – until she met George Antheil one night at a party.

At first glance, George didn't seem like a perfect inventing partner. But the duo found they had a lot in common. George had left school early and, like Hedwig, had no formal training in engineering. But, also like Hedwig, he was able to think outside of the box. He had a system that he'd used to sync pianos that he could adapt to bring Hedwig's idea to life. Together, they created a secret communication system based on frequency hopping that was met with enthusiasm. The National Inventors Council – a group of engineers themselves

– were struck by the value and originality of what Hedwig and George had created. They connected the pair with an electronics expert. When this final piece of the puzzle was solved, their idea was issued a full patent. Legitimised, they were on their way to impacting the world – and the Second World War – with their idea.

Hedwig had always known she wanted to make her mark, and while her day job was giving her a profile, she hoped that this was her chance to do something of impact with her life. More than once, she'd come close to quitting her other work and going to Washington to join the Inventors Council – but it wasn't to be that simple. Hedwig was accused of stealing the idea, of plagiarising. Others accused her of being a spy. Still, she would not be deterred.

Hedwig and George donated their invention to the National Inventors Council and, from there, it was given to the US Navy, who rejected it. Hedwig wanted to continue to develop it, but George was done. Then the patent seemingly disappeared from view. Hedwig was advised that she would make a greater contribution to the war using her beauty than her brains. Far from receiving recognition for her intellect, she was told to leave the work of inventing to the experts and go out and raise money selling war bonds instead. It was implied that this was the best way – within her realm of capabilities – to do good. Sadly, she started to believe this, too. A little of her fire went out. But, alongside a return to her day job, Hedwig was still driven to help, doing what she could on behalf of the United States and their soldiers, despite not yet being a US citizen. She raised over US$25 million – no small impact, but not what she'd had in mind when she'd set out to change the course of the war.

Hedwig (or Hedy) Lamarr was no ordinary woman. Hailed one of the most beautiful women in the world, Hedy's "day job" was as a famous film star with MGM Studios, starring in, among others, *Lady of the Tropics* (1939), *Boom Town* (1940), *H. M. Pulham, Esq.* (1941), and *White Cargo* (1942); her most celebrated role was in Paramount Pictures' *Samson and Delilah* (1949).

Despite simply wanting to stay home and invent things, Hedy's astonishing beauty hindered her from having the bigger impact she dreamed of. She was deterred from doing the work she loved and showing up in the way she wanted to contribute. Instead, Hedy came to believe that she couldn't possibly be a great inventor, that she didn't fit the box reserved for those capable of serious, game-changing innovations.

Yet the story of her frequency-hopping patent didn't end in a long-forgotten military safe. It would be revived decades later, becoming one of the technologies on which Wi-Fi, GPS and Bluetooth were all based. Again, no small impact. Just imagine what else we could have had if she had been supported instead of squashed.

•••

Anyone – even inventor-aspiring movie stars – can be a thought leader.

Thought leadership requires that we care about something enough that we're driven to think more deeply or broadly about it, and that we develop new ideas and insights. It also requires us to then use those ideas and that thinking to contribute, to help others. Many of us are doing this in the course of our work every day in the businesses we start, the movements we champion, and the services we deliver. But we're not giving ourselves the label of "thought leader". It still feels like a term that doesn't belong to us. However, as Hedy proved, you don't need to have years of training or a degree in engineering to come up with something new and incredible, or to have an impact. The dominant archetype of a thought leader describes the unicorns, but they aren't the full picture. We need a broader definition of what a thought leader is and who can be one. We need our thinking – especially the influential thinking that is "out there" – to be as good as it can be, and we need the leadership aspect – the part that makes the thinking influential – to be more accessible to more people. If we consider that our lives are ultimately the sum of the most prevalent thinking of our time, then that makes for some fairly high stakes.

Widening the possibilities for thought leadership, and welcoming new thinking and thinkers into the space, improves what I've come to call the "collective ideascape". In some ways, the collective ideascape is not dissimilar to the concept of the "zeitgeist" (translated from German to "spirit of the times"). For example, in the 1960s the zeitgeist was characterised by a cultural revolution, the rise of counterculture, emerging civil rights movements, and an anti-war sentiment.[23] Skip forward to the 1980s, and the zeitgeist centred around the rise of consumerism, materialism and technology. Or take the Renaissance period (approx. 1450–1600) with its renewed interest in classical learning and the arts, or the Age of Enlightenment (approx. 1640–1800) where we saw the rise of reason and science. The zeitgeist of today is marked by the Covid-19 pandemic, the rise of remote work and learning, an increased focus on individual freedoms and wellbeing, and growing concerns for environmental issues.

While the zeitgeist takes a broader socio-cultural view, the collective ideascape narrows down our definition to focus on the domain of thought leadership. As such, the collective ideascape is the bank of concepts or ideas we have available to draw from when we innovate and ideate, as we navigate increasing complexity and attempt to solve the vast challenges that we face as humans. The collective ideascape is the sum of the information that we encounter, the conversations that take place in the public sphere, and the shared set of beliefs, values and moral attitudes that shape the thinking and problem-solving in our society. The dominant concepts in our collective ideascape become our most well-used and therefore most often-reached-for mental models. They shape our cultural and social norms, our frames of reference, and provide the lens through which we filter our experiences. We use these lenses to make sense of what happens to us and around us. So, the better the ideascape is, the more we have to work with – and the better the solutions to the world's challenges are that we can dream up and make happen.

Lecturer and science writer Annie Murphy Paul has a rather radical way of thinking about thinking. Far removed from the brain-as-computer and brain-as-muscle metaphors that many of us are used to, Paul views the brain as more like a magpie – 'fashioning their finished products from the materials around them, weaving the bits and pieces they find into their trains of thought'.[24] As a total magpie brain myself, this analogy really resonated with me, and supported the case I was already building for the collective ideascape:

that we fashion ideas from the world around us. In the act of thinking, we're continuously drawing on resources external to our own brains and assembling and reassembling ideas as we need them. Just as the quality of the materials magpies can find determines the strength and integrity of their nests, the kinds of materials that are available to "think with" affect the quality of the ideas and solutions that we can produce. We need good ideas and solid, robust concepts to work from as we navigate modern life.

Further to this, Paul asserts that 'individual cognition is simply not sufficient to meet the challenges of a world in which information is so abundant, expertise is so specialized, and issues are so complex. In this milieu, a single mind labouring on its own is at a distinct disadvantage in solving problems or generating new ideas.'[25] Paul insists that, instead, we need to generate a sort of "group mind" replete with factual knowledge, skilled expertise, distributed mental effort and – I would add – diverse lived experiences, and the varied perspectives they bring. This is the collective ideascape, and it reinforces what we've seen already: not only do we need to be able to think well to solve the issues facing us, but we need all those who are doing great thinking to share the valuable, progress-fuelling thoughts that they have. We need to allow better thinking, from all sources, to make it to this collective ideascape, where it can then realise its potential for impact. Thought leadership is important in our world so we need to do things better; we need more great thinking being shared and more varied ways of leading with it being accepted.

Redefining thought leadership

If we are to reconsider the idea of thought leadership, then we have to start by looking at what we really mean by "thought leadership" in the first place – where the lines are drawn now. Only then can we begin to shift the boundaries and broaden the restrictive definition that many of us are walking around with. It's from there that we can evolve the field, as we've seen happen in the wider world of leadership.

Thought leadership is as simple as what it says on the tin – thinking and leadership – but it's still easy to get caught up in the hype around the term as a buzzword. We also know there has been much more emphasis previously put on the leading component than the thinking part. So, beyond the buzz, what does this combination of thought and leadership actually mean, or look like?

Thought leadership can look like speaking on stage in front of thousands of people. Starting your own TV show or YouTube channel. Becoming a lecturer or conducting significant research that receives vast media attention. Or distilling down a simple concept in a way that makes it go viral. All of these can be examples of thought leadership. But so can writing and launching a book, converting aspects of your framework into a self-led course, or launching a "train the trainer" programme to bring more of your magic into organisations via skilled facilitators. The qualities that bring all of these activities together – and delineates them as thought leadership, to my mind – are the clear conviction that something could be better, a commitment to working towards making that thing better, and a genuine and generous desire to help others move towards that version of better for themselves. Thought leadership encompasses both the ideas that have the potential to change the world for the better, and the action needed to turn that potential into reality. David Kelley, founder of IDEO and creator of the Hasso Plattner Institute of Design at Stanford, calls this "creative confidence"– that special combination of the ability to have ideas and the courage to act on them. It's both of these aspects that I'm referring to when I talk about the coupling of thought and leadership.

The first part – the thinking – is taken care of through learning, engaging with ideas, and generating new thoughts. It involves connecting with a relevant problem or challenge, and developing forward-thinking frameworks or methods that could make up a solution. It could consist of robust reading or research, ideating with others, or the evidence that's gathered through experience and when you test out what happens when your ideas meet the real world. Either way, the thinking part of thought leadership involves dedicated effort and a continual commitment to engaging in evolving your thinking, or refining your ideas, further.

Then there's the leadership part. We already know leadership, more generally, to be about inspiring and encouraging people towards shared objectives or desired outcomes. Unlocking potential and encouraging or taking your team, your clients, your company towards a better future is the name of the game for leadership. The same applies here, but we're using our ideas to do so. It might be helping others to recognise their strengths and use them more mindfully, engaging teams to reach their potential, sharing tools to support people to maintain healthy minds alongside their high performance, or any number of other initiatives that are being implemented because of people's great ideas.

Without both the thinking *and* the leadership part, you can't have impact through thought leadership. You can have ground-breaking ideas or game-changing ways of doing something, but unless you share them, then their value, and utility – and therefore their impact – will be limited. If your great ideas stay solely inside your head, they serve no-one.

For most of us who are doing the work, day-to-day, to make things better, we're constrained by our capacity and our calendars. Our impact goes only as far as those we can work with. But that's precisely what makes thought leadership appealing: it increases the impact we can have, casting our ideas further and affecting more people in positive ways.

A quieter version

I've heard it said that the true game-changers are those who stay in the shadows. They're not the ones we read about so often in the press, because they are simply getting on with being the change they want to see in the world. And this is true to an extent. There are many who are toiling away on the tough stuff and making significant progress while continuing to fly under the radar.

The real aspiration for thought leadership is not simply how loudly the ideas are being expressed, but more to do with how great thinking is made both accessible and available to benefit others. Thought leadership – as I'm defining it here – has *applicability.* It adds something, contributes practical value, and inspires people towards something being better. A bigger impact can be had with ideas that have greater reach, but what's more important is that great thinking is put out into the world in a useable format that others can derive benefit from. Do that well, at whatever decibel, and it can be one of the most meaningful and magical ways to contribute value.

Both throughout history, and today, we have come to appreciate different types of contribution – not all of which come from those who are shouting. In *Quiet,* Cain draws our attention to outstanding introverted leaders – in particular, Charles Darwin, Marie Curie, Patrick White, and Arthur Boyd – who 'created either new fields of thought or rearranged existing knowledge' and who also spent large periods of their life in solitude.[26]

But we can also look at present-day examples of incredible changemakers who aren't yet household names – like some we've worked with at Intelligent Ink. Rachel Kelly from Taylored Health – alongside her partner Luke Taylor – may be largely flying under the radar, but they are creating incredible ripples through their work. Using science and personalised data, Rachel and Luke are exploring and enhancing our human potential – helping people unlock extraordinary wellbeing and feel the best they have ever felt. Having reversed their own biological ages by 14 and 11 years, respectively, this dynamic duo are – at the time of writing – putting together a team for XPRIZE Healthspan, a seven-year $101 million global competition to revolutionise the way we approach human ageing.

Or consider the work of the charity I Have a Dream, who are demonstrating how long-term, holistic and strength-based investment in a generation of local children has a positive impact on the community and, ultimately, the wider world.

Stemming originally from the US-based movement, I Have a Dream started in Aotearoa New Zealand in 2003, and since then have supported over 2,000 Kiwi children to transform their lives, their futures and their communities. They may not be broadcasting their work far and wide, concentrating so far on incredible results in a small number of schools, but I Have A Dream are working behind the scenes to shape social and educational policy. They're showing the ways that the current model isn't working, and demonstrating the efficacy of a better one, with their social approach returning at least $3.60 for every dollar invested.

These quieter forms – whether that be developing new techniques in the arts, influencing public policy, creating new philosophies, writing profound books, or making scientific breakthroughs – still signal significant contributions. They also provide us with further proof that there's not just one way that thought leadership should be done, or only one type of person who is capable of doing it.

Hope for a way forward for thought leadership

We can look to the evolution of leadership theory to see where thought leadership needs to go next. In the 19th century, one prevailing line of thinking about leadership and history was based around what's come to be called the "Great Man" theory: the idea that history was shaped by the actions of great people – typically men – through their personal attributes and divine inspiration. The focus of this theory was on the innate characteristics of a leader. The core belief was that leaders were born, as opposed to made or trained, and that the study of great men could reveal one's own heroic side. (Some might recognise this theory's descendants even today in our hero-worship of wealthy and successful entrepreneurs, or the dominant thought leadership archetype.) Yet we risk staying stuck in our thinking about thought leadership if we continue to look at the dominant model and assume that some people simply have what it takes to participate, and others don't.

Just as leadership thinking has moved on from there, we can, too. Even as far back as the 1940s and 1950s – referred to in leadership land as the "behavioural era" – thinking had evolved to support the idea that leaders can be made or, more specifically, that particular behaviours can be learnt to ensure effective leadership. The focus shifted from born-with, inherent traits to characteristics that could be cultivated, which opened leadership up to becoming a learnt skill. Leadership was redefined to become something you *did* more than something you *were* – an important distinction as far as our thinking about thought leadership goes. However, it's where leadership went next that brings me the most hope in terms of improving thought leadership.

A growing field in academic research and leadership theory in the latter part of the 20th century made moves towards authenticity and a focus on "realness". Perhaps this was a way of the pendulum swinging back from learned leadership behaviours towards innate character once again, but the emphasis was different this time. Authentic leadership encourages people to lead in a real, genuine and sincere way that is true to who they are as individuals.[27] This is a very different approach to acting the part, or adopting a persona based on the behaviours that leaders are expected to demonstrate.

Authentic leadership advocates reject the idea that leaders ought to adopt a persona different than their own. This opens up the world of leadership to allow more styles to be effective. It broadens out what a leader can be, and puts the focus more on whether the person is successfully achieving outcomes than ticking any pre-prescribed boxes. This is absolutely what we want for thought leadership, too: more relaxed criteria and a broader scope when it comes to what works. We also want any evaluations of success to be based on actual performance, and not on proficiency at performing.

It should not be a bold or countercultural idea that we judge thought leaders on real results and their impact, over how well they play a part that looks good or comes across well. Tomas Chamorro-Premuzic, a professor of business psychology at University College London, echoes this challenge in *Why Do So Many Incompetent Men Become Leaders?*, where he asserts that it's not just gender bias that holds women back from leadership and sees incompetent men floating to the top, but also because of a broken bridge between actual leadership talent and our assumptions about it. As he puts it: 'There is a world of difference between the personality traits and behaviours it takes to be *chosen* as a leader and the traits and skills you need to *be able* to lead effectively.'[28]

The same exists for thought leadership. We've got a fundamental disconnect between what we think we need in order to be a successful thought leader, and the skills and behaviours actually required to build thought leadership. This mismatch is holding back too many potential – yet reluctant – thought leaders.

There is so much space for more, and for different. Many of the qualities that people see as making them ill-suited to thought leadership are actually the presently under-valued superpowers that we need to make things better. And that's exciting. There are a huge number of potential contributors that we'll be able to hear from, but only when we start embracing, celebrating and opening up to the more aligned and authentic styles of those who have – until now – been held back from doing this work. I hope that one of them will be you. Together we will do away with the prescribed boxes of the dominant model of thought leadership and create the space for more people to have an impact in their own unique ways.

So far:

We know that too-narrow ideas about thought leadership are holding us back, and that's a problem when there are vast challenges that we need to overcome.

Not only do we need to be able to think well to solve the issues facing us, but we need all those who are doing great thinking and great work to share the valuable, progress-fuelling thoughts that they have.

If we go back to basics, we see that thought leadership is still – at its heart – about thinking and leadership; having ideas that could change the world for the better, and then taking the action required to turn that potential into a reality, while inspiring others along with you.

In this way, thought leadership is a valid and valuable way to contribute to our collective ideascape – the bank of concepts or ideas that we draw from as we ideate, innovate and problem-solve. Yet we will only realise the potential of this if we share more great thinking, and accept more varied ways of leading.

There is hope. We've seen the field of leadership open up and evolve its thinking and practices – from innate traits to learned behaviours and then back towards authenticity. Now it's time for thought leadership to similarly do so.

CHAPTER 3

Blind spots and biases

It was 10:06 a.m. but we were yet to get underway. People were still trickling into the meeting room. We were on the seventh floor of Lifewise's central-city head office, looking out over Myers Park and watching the bustle of Auckland's busy Queen Street down below. A local social development organisation, Lifewise is one of many in our not-for-profit niche that we have helped with copywriting and communications. On this particular Thursday morning, I was there to talk to their key workers in the hopes of finding a story that could form the basis of a donor letter. I hadn't been able to get what I needed this time around from the marketing and fundraising team, so I had decided to approach those on the front-line for a compelling story that might encourage the organisation's supporters to open both their hearts and their wallets.

Only three of the five key workers who had agreed to the meeting were present yet. 'We'll just wait a couple more minutes for the others,' I said, looking around the room with what I hoped was a reassuring smile on my face. The three social workers who had arrived were shifting nervously in their seats, surprisingly subdued in their conversations despite the rare opportunity for close contact with their colleagues all physically in the office together. 'You don't need to be nervous,' I added.

My platitudes did little to lighten the mood.

In the next minute or so, the other two women we were waiting for bustled in, overflowing folders, and steaming, just-balanced cups of tea in hand. As they sat down around the vast conference table, I readied myself to begin.

After some welcomes, I started. 'I know you're not used to contributing to the marketing stuff. And I realise it might feel as though I have taken you away from the important projects you are otherwise working on this morning, so thank you for being here. My aim is most definitely not to draw this out …'

Although they had been briefed by their marketing colleague, I explained again that I was trying to pull together a story that highlighted, to those outside the organisation, the incredible work that they all did. 'Oh gosh, that feels like a lot of pressure,' one of the women laughed. 'I hope we don't prove to be a waste of time!' another added. I promised them that they most certainly would not. But I also resigned myself to the fact that this might take a bit more coaxing on my part.

I explained that they didn't need to pluck just the right anecdote from their minds or memories and tell it to me perfectly so that I could write it into a donor letter verbatim. I asked them instead to simply share some of the things that they were working on currently, such as the cases they had open that week. I reassured them that if they just talked freely, I could craft what I needed from there. And, of course, they would have the chance to read and approve anything before it was used. This worked to lower the stakes for them, and, after looking at each other to see who would venture to speak first, one of them started to talk.

She told me about a young pregnant woman who had been sleeping on the streets. They had just managed to secure safe housing for her. This key worker was currently helping the expectant mum to get settled, as it was only a couple of weeks before her baby was due. The colleague seated to her left at the table then shared about the additional wraparound support that the organisation was providing to this young woman. This was in his domain. He enthusiastically detailed how this would continue alongside her throughout the next part of her journey to ensure that she and her baby could remain in their home.

After a short pause, another woman at the table shared what she had learnt just that week following her check-in with the team at Merge Café, one of the organisation's welcoming and inclusive community spaces. Her report was full of stories of people who were taking proactive steps to overcome trauma, addiction and other challenges with the backing of people who believed in them. As she spoke, I could hear how proud she was of the progress these people were making in turning their lives around.

Slowly and haltingly, a picture of what these key workers do started to emerge, along with the incredible impact that they have on behalf of an organisation whose mission they so obviously believed in. Going into the meeting, I had thought I knew that the work the organisation did was significant.

Hearing first-hand the lives that Lifewise were touching, and the passion their people clearly had, was moving. I told them as much. Several of them blushed. 'But that's just a normal week for us,' one said. 'Par for the course,' another added, nodding.

•••

It can be difficult to see that what we do day-to-day is extraordinary, just as it's normal to feel reluctant about putting our work and our ideas out into the world. Not only does sharing our work and our thinking more widely call for us to expose something of ourselves to others, but it often requires us to wrestle with our critical internal voice. This necessitates vulnerability. What the Lifewise team were describing reflected a standard, run-of-the-mill week for them, yet it was very far from what many others do in a normal week. And although it was difficult for them to recognise their work as being remarkable, the stories that they were sharing were extraordinary.

There's a proverb that suggests that fish will be the last ones to discover water, immersed in it as they are. We tend to take for granted what we are swimming in. One of my fabulous friends and clients, Daria Williamson, similarly often shares a quote that she's collected somewhere along the line: 'It's hard to read the label when you're inside the bottle.'

The team at Lifewise were doing great work, but they were reluctant to own it as such, or to share it further, even when I was asking them to do so. They're not alone. While it might appear that others don't worry about whether they have enough value to offer, it's overwhelmingly common to feel resistance when it comes to thought leadership. When you are playing big and wanting to have a positive impact on the world, you will be pushing yourself into new territory.

The expert's blind spot

It's normal for work to seem largely unremarkable to the ones doing it. Whether helping people find homes, lead their teams better, do work they are proud of, disrupt an industry that needs improving, build businesses that work for them, or any other number of better outcomes that people are pursuing, people do amazing work but often struggle to see themselves as experts.

Through my work, I speak with incredibly clever and competent people who claim that they don't know enough, or haven't figured it all out yet, so therefore they're not ready to make proactive moves to increase their impact. I call this the "over-thinking" brand of reluctance. Meanwhile, others believe that they aren't doing anything out of the ordinary – certainly nothing that anyone else wouldn't also choose to do, or be able to do, if faced with the same situation. This latter group are experiencing what I refer to as the "nothing special" reluctance. We're going to explore more about how our critical inner voice can derail us shortly; however, it's not only an internal block that reluctant thought leaders are encountering. Sure, there's humility at play here (albeit probably over-played), however it's also a case that, like the fish not recognising that its surrounded by water, the perspective we're taking when looking at our own work makes it very difficult to see its value clearly.

This blind spot to our own brilliance comes from the all-too-common "curse of knowledge" or "curse of expertise". This cognitive bias occurs when we assume that others have the same information, background and understanding that we possess. When you have learnings, experience and expertise in an area, that thing becomes much clearer in your mind. We get more proficient and familiar with ideas that we've spent a lot of time thinking about, or concepts that we've spent a lot of time practising or applying. This increased familiarity then brings with it comfort and clarity – and when something becomes really comfortable or crystal-clear, it starts to appear obvious. Certain. Definite. Simple. We reason: surely everyone else knows this? We lack empathy for what it is really like to be outside our own heads. It may also be, as is the case at Lifewise, that we're surrounded by other expert peers who are doing much the same things that we are. The overall bar is high, so we're simply sitting on it, alongside – and certainly not ahead of – others.

Either way, as the result of our immersion day-to-day, the things we're doing get normalised and new discoveries get relatively seamlessly assimilated with all our other working knowledge. Things we learn quickly come to seem like something we've always known. They get taken for granted, and we can no longer imagine *not* knowing them. This reinforces the assumption (conscious or not) that others must know what we know, or be able to do what we can do, too. As a result of all of this, our knowledge loses a bit of its special status – if it ever really had any in the first place.

But what about the over-confidence effect?

Of course, not everybody struggles to see how special, unique or valuable their contribution to the world is. You can likely call to mind at least a handful of people who seem to have an overly inflated sense of this. The over-confidence effect is another well-documented cognitive bias that sees people's subjective confidence in their own ability as much greater than their objective or actual performance. In other words, they overestimate their knowledge and abilities in a certain area.

We all like to think we're immune from this, and our frequent dances with our negative internal voice, and our experiences of under-confidence, suggest to us that we are. Yet, even with that considered, we are all still likely to overrate our skills and talents in at least some areas. Decades of research suggests that we tend to assume we are better than we actually are when it comes to a wide-ranging list of competencies or characteristics.[29] Professors Alexander Freund and Nadine Kasten looked at over 20,000 people's self-rated intelligence scores against their measured intelligence test scores and found less than a 10 percent overlap between how smart people think they are and how smart they actually are.[30] We're not always great at judging our own proficiencies, in other words – especially as this finding has since been replicated for a wide range of other abilities and competence domains.

You may have heard the infamous quip that 80 percent of people think that they are "above average" drivers.[31] As funny and statistically impossible as this is, this research isn't intended to further shake your self-belief, at least not as far as making you doubt yourself more. Instead it's intended to disrupt your belief that you have an accurate gauge on your value and skills.

Despite the prevalence of over-confidence, the overwhelming majority of people who I talk to experience the blind spot that makes it difficult to recognise their own gifts and talents, especially when it comes to thought leadership. It's hard to get a real read. I find that people are so wary of falling prey to their egos that they take it too far to the other extreme, and end up downplaying the value they are delivering.

Self-awareness can help, but many of the people I'm talking about who are experiencing this expertise blind spot are relatively self-aware. Self-awareness does tend to increase a little with talent, or as we develop more proficiency in a particular area, but even that has its limits. Social psychologists have found that – alarmingly – experts and clueless people tend not to differ very much in their self-perceived abilities.[32] We all like to think we are competent and proficient. Bertrand Russell, the British mathematical philosopher and Nobel Laureate, famously said that 'the fundamental cause of the trouble is that in the modern world the stupid are cocksure while the intelligent are full of doubt'.[33] And he's not wrong. Less-skilled individuals tend to make the least accurate evaluations of their talents, while it's common for the most competent to exhibit more self-doubt.

As we'll see in Chapter 6 when we look at uncertainty, the expertise blind spot can bring benefits, like greater preparation, continuous learning, and conscientious fact-checking. However, it is still sad that so many people walk around struggling to see their own brilliance, and it's especially a waste when reluctant thought leaders fail to contribute because it's so difficult for them to see the value they could bring if they did.

To this day, one of the most special aspects of the work that I get to do is showing people how extraordinary they are, and how valuable their work and thinking really is. I do this largely by looking at the facts: I help them to block out much of the internal and external noise to build an evidence-based view of their expertise. This is something that you can do for yourself, too. It is possible to reconcile the two extremes, and arrive at an accurate assessment – one that enables you to stop diminishing what you have to offer and start overcoming your reluctance. The fact-based picture that you form then becomes the foundation needed – your solid ground, so to speak – for building thought leadership. An evidence-based view of your value is the place that you need to be standing to feel confident enough to put your ideas, and therefore yourself, out there.

However, it is just the start.

The foundation for overcoming reluctance

There are four aspects to overcoming reluctance when it comes to thought leadership.

They're not so much sequential steps that you will pass through once and move on from, but strategies that you can tap into as you need. Some, or potentially all of these, will be things that you will have to dance with many times, but it's from here that your thought leadership, and ultimately your impact, will grow. Let's take a look.

1. **Build an evidence-based view of the value that you are, or could be, contributing.**

The first place to look is right in front of you. Here, we're trying to move away from solely subjective judgements – or your feelings about what you're doing – and look towards more objective assessments. We're starting to gather the facts, the evidence of your value. This may sound daunting, but don't shy away from this. To begin, consider: Are you already doing something that's contributing towards making something better?

Potential thought leaders not only have clear conviction that something could be better, but they're doing something about it. Thinking about a problem, and coming up with potential solutions, isn't quite enough – at least, not in an age of ideas where information is so abundant. In the past few decades, thought leadership has come to depend on applying knowledge and information with experience, testing it in action, bringing our own stories and perspectives, and adding something new. This is the step beyond the information itself holding all the power, and a move towards using it to create value. It is also absolutely required if we want to actually change anything. All the thinking in the world counts for little if you're not prepared to act on any of it.

The Lifewise team certainly had that going for them. Far from sitting around and lamenting the challenges that the most vulnerable members of our communities were facing, they were out there improving freedom, choice and equity. Believing that impact consists of going beyond the immediate needs of people living with hardship, their work addresses the root causes of social issues and supports people to turn their lives around for good. And the impact was right there, present in their stories and their statistics. That year, over 20,000 nourishing meals had been served in the haven of Merge Café. 108 people had been supported into temporary housing, and a further 63 into permanent housing. 196 people had received specialised treatment for mental health and addiction.[34] There was no shortage of action.

You need to be doing *something* to have the potential for thought leadership – however, from the outset, this doesn't need to mean proactively and strategically building thought leadership. Not yet anyway. Doing something, at least to begin with, simply means that you are acting on your ideas. Kon Apostolopoulos and his business Fresh Biz Solutions, from their base in Colorado, have been helping businesses to achieve their strategic goals and further enhance their financial results through the power of their people for more than two decades. Kon was able to help one of his main clients, a multi-million-dollar construction company, to retain their talent *and* grow their employees by 25 percent – even in the midst of the challenges of the Covid-19 pandemic and the Great Resignation that followed. This was no small feat, but it was an essential step in enabling the organisation to achieve that year's record revenues of 50 percent growth from the year prior.

Closer to home, Kiwi-based Daria Williamson – whose work we are going to look at more in the next chapter – has bought her unique strengths-based approach to more than 250 people via a combination of one-on-one coaching and small group workshop sessions. In opening people's eyes to their strengths and what is in their "zone of genius", Daria makes her clients feel more energised and productive, more authentic, and more intentional. What she is doing is truly game-changing for others' work and lives.

And finally, there's Ellen Joan Ford, the fiercely ambitious Kiwi behind the #WorkSchoolHours movement. Before writing her book *#WorkSchoolHours: A Revolution for Parents, Workplaces and the World*, Ellen had already spoken in front of tens of thousands of people about her framework for making work better. She had worked closely with the New Zealand Army and, according to Major General John Boswell, DSD, Chief of NZ Army, 'she has significantly influenced how Army is now approaching a range of diversity and inclusion challenges, particularly those that relate to gender inclusiveness'.[35] Not only that, but Ellen has also concurrently been bringing her expertise and innovative thinking to a nationwide leadership development project for New Zealand's largest sector – the food and fibre sector – which employs over 330,000 people. Again, no shortage of action.

Like these Intelligent Ink clients, and so many others who we have a chance to meet and talk to every day, you are likely also contributing to making something better either through a business that you've started, services you deliver, a movement you are championing, or value that you're contributing to the world in some way. If you look closely, there are examples of excellence, impact, positive difference and people using their expertise to encourage others towards better outcomes happening every day.

This is where the leading part of thought leadership needs to start. Action is where the rubber hits the road. This isn't only true for thought leadership, but also for the world of leadership more generally. We hear all the platitudes about leading by example and leading from the front, about how leaders ought to model the behaviours they want to see or the change they want to inspire, and about the respect afforded to hands-on leaders who truly know what their teams are going through because they are also elbows-deep in experiencing it. In the world of thought leadership, the same applies: *doing* provides the opportunity for leading. Taking the initiative and giving something a try enables thinkers to test and refine their ideas, gather evidence, and build confidence in what they are thinking as they learn more. It allows us close enough to a problem to be part of the solution.

We're going to look more at the value of experience shortly, but for now it's enough to understand that it's important to *do* something and to be starting to see some promising results. It's here that you take the first step towards getting an accurate assessment of what you have to offer. Look at the impact that you are already having with your ideas, across a range of situations, and the results you are getting. Perhaps you can see that you're smashing it in that domain – but, at the very least, are there little glimmers of success that you've got evidence of? This is what you should be judging your effectiveness by, not other arbitrary measures. Be wary about comparing your impact to that of others or the examples here also; everyone's version, and everyone's mission, is different.

When you think of success, it does not need to mean considerable commercial returns, although those are a good indicator that you have something that others perceive to be valuable. Nor does it need to mean that you're receiving awards or rocketing levels of recognition. It simply means that you are getting closer to the outcome that you are working towards, that your thinking is being effectively applied, and that you are making a difference.

As a result of the work of Debbie Schultz and her team at BlueSkyMinds, more than 50 organisations across New

Zealand and Australia have enhanced their wellbeing strategies and are supporting their people to maintain healthy minds alongside their high performance. Hundreds of people – spanning sectors as diverse as healthcare, insurance, accounting, manufacturing, law, banking, technology, tertiary education and government – are now experiencing less overwhelm (on average a 20 percent decrease in self-reported stress), and an increased ability to handle pressure (on average a 15 percent increase in resilience) and increased productivity (up by an average of 40 percent) following their programmes. The ripple effect of this is huge and reaches far beyond these people's day jobs. Not only are they performing better at work, but they are happier, too, which means they are showing up differently in their relationships also. There is massive value in what Debbie and her team are doing, and so many others are getting the benefits of it. Like Debbie, potential thought leaders have a conviction that something could be better. So, whether you're creating a small or a significant measure of change that demonstrates that hypothesis to be correct, then that is success.

Evidence of your success is the starting seed for confidence. Genuine or right-sized confidence should be based on actual achievements, experience, and results. Assessments based on nothing other than self-belief can border towards arrogance or – at the other extreme – keep us stuck playing small. Assessments grounded in evidence give us a truer picture. However, I understand that this exercise might feel daunting, or it's possible that you don't really know where to start. Not many of us have a beautifully branded organisational infographic that presents all of our key outcomes for the year. Further to that, we don't often think about the implications of our actions. Yet, small actions can absolutely lead to big outcomes.

How many stories have you heard where some small gesture – some throwaway action or comment that was quickly forgotten by the person who did it – went on to change the course of somebody's life? Take National Football League (NFL) star, Jerry Rice, a three-time Superbowl Champion and career leader in most statistical categories for the wide-receiver position he played.[36] Jerry didn't even play football, or any sports, initially in high school. That all changed when he was caught cutting class with a friend. Panicked, he sprinted away from the assistant principal's wrath, unwittingly showcasing his speed. His punishment by the school was to try out for the football team.

Or what about German diplomat Heinrich Albert who, in 1915, fatefully fell asleep on a train while holding a briefcase containing espionage plans? Jolted awake at his stop, Albert fuzzily found that his briefcase was missing; it had been seized by a Secret Service Agent who was tailing him.[37] This took place at a time when the United States was still neutral, opting to stay out of the war that was setting Europe ablaze. However, the contents of the briefcase proved that Germany was trying to manipulate the American people. When the documents were leaked to the press, outrage ensued, and America joined the First World War. Massive ramifications – all because a spy couldn't stay awake.

Most of us don't have the high stakes of spies and secret agents surrounding the work we do, but the fact remains that what you do matters, and that sometimes the seemingly little things can become the big things. Even though some of your actions may be hard to quantify, there will be evidence of your impact out there. You may need to lift yourself "out of the water", so to speak, or adopt a little hindsight in order to look for it. Talk to those who you work with and see what they say about what you are doing. Yes, their feedback is subjective, but you're not looking for their perceptions or judgements about how you're showing up, rather the outcomes or results that you are achieving with them, or the results that they are achieving following your work with them.

2. Value your experience

Understanding that your contribution is making something better is one thing, but it's another thing to truly value the experience that you have and continue to gain.

So many of the potential thought leaders who I talk to, or the thought leaders who I work with, continue to experience imposter syndrome – that feeling that they don't rightly belong – even though they are already successfully doing the thing that they do in their little (or even large) corner of the world and achieving an impact. Some of them protest that they don't have a degree in their topic or, in some cases, any type of formal qualification. Others acknowledge that while they may be a professional or a practitioner, they don't have a particular title that they perceive they need. These all signify labels, and none of them are real prerequisites. There are people with no titles who, in some arenas, are doing a hell of a lot more than people with the highest-ranked titles. Similarly, there are people who never went to university or who didn't even finish high school who have a lot of valuable things that they could teach to some of those with much more formal education. So, this isn't about badges per se. Instead, it's about action and outcomes, and about understanding that what you have to offer has tremendous value.

While I am in no way discounting education – the acquisition of knowledge is incredibly important, after all – there is more than one way to acquire it. The entire approach that we are taking to thought leadership here highlights the need to value different paths. Structured or formal education may be a foot in the door, or proof of a particular skill, but expertise is not built on academics alone. We need only look to the likes of Bill Gates, Richard Branson, Steve Jobs, Coco Chanel and Mary Kay Ash – all of whom either dropped out of high school or never went to university to see that, while certifications may validate learning, they aren't everything. Furthermore, all the knowledge in the world doesn't really hold much weight until it is tried out or acted upon.

We're often quick to convince ourselves that we aren't expert enough to pursue a greater impact. 'Immeasurable contributions are lost because many women think traditional expertise is the only kind of legitimate qualification,' Mohr reminds us in *Playing Big*.[38] Of course, it's not just women. Too many of us under-value the experience that we have, drawing unfair and untrue conclusions that we can't really be an expert. The thing is that we don't tend to hold the same judgements for others; we love listening to insightful perspectives based on people's personal experiences. As Mohr explains, insiders (or 'survivors', in her words) have an edge – they have the lived experience that the experts study, which means they often have insights that some of the experts don't, noting:

> They frequently bring forward neglected perspectives and a reality check on the expert's take. They have the power to inspire, not just to inform, and they tend to bring a greater sense of passion and compassion to the work at hand … what they have to share is more than enough. The contribution they make is all the more unique, all the more potent because they have a personal story to share rather than the official experts' take.[39]

Not only that, but there is also a huge array of valuable things that people learn through doing. Immersion in doing or practising while learning allows people to gain both propositional (fact-filled) and procedural (actionable) knowledge. And although it can be harder to quantify hands-on learning, it combines cognitive, emotional, social and behavioural elements in a way that makes it both comprehensive and effective. That's why we get trainee nurses on the wards, teacher trainees into classrooms and apprentice builders on-site before their qualifications are complete. The learnings to be gained on the job are invaluable to the process of becoming an expert.

I often tell people that Aotearoa New Zealand has a less mature thought leadership industry than those that exist in other parts of the world, but I've come to appreciate that it has a specific and advantageous edge, too. We have, at this stage at least, very few "career" thought leaders (i.e. those who make thought leadership their entire job). Instead, those thought leaders we do have balance the work of building thought leadership with delivering on their ideas through the work that they do. This may stem from our smaller scale; our organisations, being often smaller in size than those of our international peers, require all hands on deck. Or perhaps the fact that Kiwis, culturally, value proven results and experience in building trust. (We're also a little more allergic than others to posturing, which shows that we want our leaders to talk the talk *and* walk the walk.) Either way, I have long believed that practising professionals make better thought leaders than "talking heads" because they are actively delivering their ideas. Practising professionals are elbows-deep and have fertile testing grounds to continuously improve their ideas. They're also able to remain much closer to, and more connected with, their working theories and evidence. Experience in doing the thing enables people to acquire real knowledge, as opposed to merely espousing what they think, have been told, or have read.

This idea of "real" knowledge comes from the late Charlie Munger, an American businessman, investor and philanthropist, who differentiated between real knowledge and what he called "chauffeur knowledge".[40] For Munger, real knowledge is gained by people who have committed a large amount of time and effort to understanding a topic. Maybe they have a degree or certifications in the subject, but structured education is not a requirement. More importantly, real knowledge is backed by extensive first-hand experience, and this is what distinguishes our practising professionals.

The second type – chauffeur knowledge – is presented by people who have learnt to put on a show. This is what we are often subject to in the "talking head" mode of thought leadership or, at times, what we encounter with the sage on the stage. Chauffeur knowledge may not even be the person's own understanding; they may simply be reeling off eloquent words by way of a well-practised script or via a few choice soundbites. Chauffeur knowledge is often espoused by slick deliverers, but when they've spent all their time honing the presentation of the ideas, there isn't always the same effort put into actually evolving or stress-testing the thinking itself. It's all package and no punch. The result is, often enough, statements that might sound good but in actuality contain very little substance – something my colleague Dave Taylor refers to as 'the arguments that fall over in a stiff breeze'. What they're lacking is robust thought and lived experience to back them up.

It can be difficult to spot and separate true knowledge from chauffeur knowledge out in the wild, as many of the channels that we receive information via don't allow sufficient scrutiny. If we are allowed to scratch the surface or dive a little deeper, the cracks start to show in chauffeur knowledge though. Real knowledge is backed by stories and case studies that have been experienced first-hand. There's obvious depth and breadth there when you start asking questions. Simple stuff, really.

While the Lifewise team didn't feel prepared to present a polished highlight reel of their work to me, it didn't take a lot of digging to discover that they had more than enough real-life stories to demonstrate their vast experience and expertise in tackling challenging social issues. It was unclear, in our brief interaction, how many of the key workers were, for example, tertiary-qualified (it didn't ever occur to me to ask!) – but this in no way detracted from the incredible work that this team were doing, nor lessened the impact that they were having. Their experience was more than delivering the goods.

3. Acknowledge and accept your inner critic as a constant companion

There's no way to explore steps like the two preceding ones without coming face-to-face with that pesky imposter syndrome. I have no doubt that your experience of the cautionary and sometimes-cruel voice inside your head feels intensely personal and unique to you, yet I can assure you that everyone has some version of one. Every single person I talk to experiences some form of reluctance, including those who are, by all external measures, already successfully putting their ideas out into the world and leading with their thinking. They can all identify aspects that are holding them back from either building, or really believing in the success of, their thought leadership. Whether well down the road to thought leadership or still just thinking about starting on it, they all have beliefs about themselves or the world around them that hold them back. Me included. I continuously doubt whether I have anything useful to say, whether I've done enough work to back up what I'm saying, or whether I'm ready to put it out there yet. (I've lost count of how many re-writes I've done on this book by now!)

Not only could I see the doubts and hesitation all over the faces of the Lifewise team who I had gathered around the table that day, but I have never – prior to that, or since – met a client or colleague who hasn't grappled with some form of self-doubt. My job has long been to help people over their internal hurdles (and dig in to try to overcome them myself), while also encouraging the activities that broaden our idea of what thought leadership looks like and can be.

In *The War of Art: Break Through the Blocks and Win Your Inner Creative Battles,* Steven Pressfield labels the 'tricky enemy' inside all of us that sabotages our dreams as capital-R 'Resistance'. In the book's Introduction, he refers to it as 'the most toxic force on the planet' and believes it to be the source of our fears, doubts, excuses and poor habits, and also 'the root of more unhappiness than poverty, disease and erectile dysfunction'. Resistance seems to be an irrefutable law of Nature. Any time you try to move something that's stationary and put it into motion, you have to overcome resistance. So, take comfort from the fact that the doubts, worries and reluctance you are feeling are all completely normal. Some may also say that they're necessary.

Dr Bex Bell – author of *Inner Critic to Inner Coach: How to Heal the Impostor Syndrome, End Self-Sabotage and Own Your Greatness*, and a client who I also consider a friend – has a kinder take on our inner voice than Pressfield, referring to it instead as our 'inner critic'. Bex explains that not only is an inner critic a universally human thing to have, but it also serves a functional purpose: it's hard-wired into our biology, and develops as a form of protection. Our human brains care, above all else, about our survival, which is why they're extra good at detecting threats that could compromise our safety. While we no longer face the same daily dangers as our hunter-gatherer ancestors, our modern lives are stressful when it comes to social threats. 'That's why we naturally default to finding all the ways we're "not good enough",' Bex's book details.

> From a survival perspective, not measuring up could mean being cut off from our survival needs of love, connection, belonging and acceptance. We need to be highly attuned to detecting if we're falling short compared to others so we can correct our behaviour and stay in favour with our clan.[41]

It's little wonder that our brains develop a negativity bias, and it's not your fault that you have self-critical thoughts; a small army of over-protective inner critics has developed to protect you from loss and pain. This is why your inner critic tends to get more persistent, even a little shouty, when you're really stretching yourself, when you're trying to do something great, different, or new. Pushing yourself beyond the normal and the comfortable heightens the stakes. Putting yourself, and by extension, your ideas, out into the world on a bigger scale falls into this category for most people. In *Playing Big,* Mohr refers to these moments as when 'we've just woken the sleeping guard at the edge of our comfort zone.'[42] The appearance of our inner critic should be exciting when we think about it that way: it's a clue that we're on the cusp of something. Yet, it doesn't usually feel exciting to us at the time, and we're the only ones who know it's there.

That's one of the other insidious points about our inner critics: they're "inner". Because we largely conceal these critical voices and the mean things they say to us from the outside world, it's easy to assume other people aren't walking around constantly arguing with theirs. They are, though; we've all got one. Arianna Huffington – author of 15 books, co-founder of *The Huffington Post* and founder of *Thrive Global* – confesses that she has what she calls 'the anxious roommate' in her head, who tells her all the things she's doing wrong and all the ways she could fail.[43] This is despite the fact that Huffington is, by most people's measures, hugely successful.

Similarly, one of my long-standing clients and friends Suzi McAlpine – keynote speaker, executive coach to many of the country's most successful CEOs, and author of both the bestselling book *Beyond Burnout* and the award-winning blog *The Leader's Digest* – admits that she struggles with her 'strident' inner critic every day. 'When people introduce me at speaking events, I cringe – thinking that I don't deserve the way they're introducing me. I think that there are so many people who are so much more than me. While I know on some level that voice is there to protect me, it makes it difficult for me to accept any form of praise,' Suzi shared with me. Yet Suzi's calendar books out months in advance with speaking engagements and she has an enviable waitlist for her services. She's created passive streams of income and reached the well-leveraged stage with her business and her thought leadership that many aspire to. (And I know that she will cringe when she sees that I've written this about her!)

It's sometimes hard to reconcile what successful people are saying about their inner critic with the way that we see those same people. Pure SEO founder and CEO Richard Conway is another case in point: when I spoke to him for this book, he admitted that he, too, experiences 'huge self-doubt,' often second-guesses himself, and questions his own ability – despite plentiful external markers of success. 'I haven't slept properly in my 15 years in business,' Richard laughs. 'There's always something keeping me up at night. I often lie there worrying, "What if I'm wrong?" and "What haven't I seen?" or "Am I shifting fast enough? Hard enough? *Too* hard?"' This is all despite the fact that Richard heads up multiple digital agencies, including one that spans three countries and has collected multiple awards. Like me, Richard believes it's natural to have self-doubt, but he also believes it keeps him on his toes.

It's an attitude shared by the formidable Mark Hayes. A superstar in the marketing and business world, Mark has moved from corporate roles to founding, growing and selling three of his own businesses before moving back into the corporate world. His career has seen him mentor and support start-ups, deliver keynote speeches on international stages, win awards for strategy, and collaborate with leaders and teams across North America, China, Australia, Japan and Aotearora New Zealand. Yet Mark similarly admits to an internal 'I suck, I suck, I suck' loop, as he words it, as well as a challenging case of 'comparisonitis', and frequent feelings that he's not good enough and that what he's doing isn't good enough yet either. 'I don't tend to take others' criticisms as hard as I take my own,' Mark admitted to me in conversation. 'Now I have what I call my folder of screw-ups where I store examples of public people – those who are at the top of their game and well-respected – who have made or admitted errors. It's there as proof that I'm not alone and that everyone makes mistakes.'

So self-doubt still lurks loudly, even for those we view as successful – even for those who seem to have every reason to be confident. I would argue that it is present for these people precisely because they are pushing further than they otherwise might think they could go. As Mohr explains it, people 'grapple with self-doubt *because* they are playing big, regularly exposing themselves to criticism and visible failures and expressing their unique ideas and leadership in the world'.[44] We're going to feel this way as we venture our ideas and ourselves out there. Accompaniment by your inner critic is natural and in no way a sign that you are unqualified, going too far, or veering out of your lane. More likely it means that you are doing, or are on your way to doing, something spectacular.

Wherever extraordinary things have been or are being achieved, there's evidence of people progressing past their limiting internal voice. As Pressfield puts it: 'Defeating Resistance is like giving birth. It seems absolutely impossible until you remember that women have been pulling it off successfully, with support and without, for fifty million years.'[45] And while I love that analogy, I would argue we don't actually need to defeat it – that is likely a fruitless pursuit. If Resistance is an inbuilt biological necessity, defeating it would be akin to amputating a limb.

A less adversarial and more productive approach to aim for is acceptance. As Bex told me: 'It's very hard to deal with something in a healthy way if we're treating it like the enemy.' Instead, we can accept that this negative and nagging companion is going to be with us through some of our most challenging times, and welcome it as an over-protective, if misguided, friend. Invite it along for the journey.

Acceptance may seem to signal passivity, resignation, or giving up, but it can also be powerful. Understanding why your inner critic is here, and what it's trying to do, helps its tricks lose some of their power. It helps you to be better able to choose your actions and reactions despite that voice piping up. I know a lot of people – Bex's clients and beyond – who find this reframing of their inner critic freeing. If we acknowledge that some form of critical inner voice is a given, we no longer need to stay frozen to the spot, hoping, wishing, or waiting for it to vanish before we can get started. You can be scared and still move forward.

Anaïs Nin's poem 'Le Risque' beautifully describes exactly this moment. Translated to English, it reads: 'And the day came/when the risk/of staying clasped/in a bud/became more painful/than the risk/it took/to blossom.'

The people who do amazing things don't do them without a negative internal voice. They do them with their inner critic tagging along. And they do them because they simply can't tolerate doing nothing.

4. Find your fire. Care enough to do the thing, even though you are scared

There's a critical difference between those who change the world and those who don't – and I hope you're beginning to see by now that it isn't what you might have originally thought. The difference is not some magical concoction of confidence, competence and connections that has paved the way for those who have succeeded. Nor is it the case that those who do great things fail to experience fear, doubt or reluctance. The difference is that the people who do incredible things *care enough to act anyway*. A reluctant thought leader is not simply anyone and everyone who is not currently doing the work to build thought leadership. Rather, they're the people with fire, clear conviction, and courage; they see that something could be better and are fighting for it. In *The Song of Significance*, Seth Godin describes courage not as the absence of fear, but instead, as 'a willingness to do things that are so important they're worth doing even (especially) when we're feeling the fear'.[46] That's what our thought leaders experience.

Those who make an impact, who really change something, are called to do so and simply can't ignore the call. It might sound lofty to refer to thought leadership as a calling, but consider it in these more practical terms: many of the thought leaders we see really moving the needle and driving us forward have, somewhere along the way, been a bit pissed off. At the very least, they've been disappointed. Not necessarily in a negative way, because they're not victims. They're not just sitting there and thinking about how something is not good enough. Instead, they're doing something about it. They're using their disillusionment to fuel them towards finding a solution.

Every thought leader I've encountered still had that voice that told them they're not smart enough, qualified enough, experienced enough, confident enough, *good-at-X* enough, so it's okay that you do, too. However, those who are making an impact have seen a way to avoid something that was tripping people up or limiting lives or businesses and they simply couldn't sit aside. They couldn't tolerate the wasted opportunity if they left things as they were. And so they were carried forward by the fierce energy that comes when you care about what you're doing. This is what you, too, will draw from.

Suzi McAlpine explained to me that this is how she's managed, despite her inner critic: 'I've learnt to thank it and then tell it to be quiet. If I don't tell it to be quiet, it stops me from doing the things that are important.' It's despite the companionship of her negative internal voice, then, that Suzi has done the things she's done – written a book, created a scalable programme, published valuable and eagerly-awaited content each fortnight on her blog, and ignited better leadership for so many Kiwi organisations.

Similarly, it's despite self-doubt and second-guessing that Richard Conway has grown his businesses, lectured for the Marketing Association, contributed for years a monthly column about digital marketing and entrepreneurship to industry magazines, written the first certified search engine optimisation (SEO) course for Aotearoa New Zealand universities, and published a book *How to Get to the Top of Google.* 'I'm still terrified every time I do anything public-facing, when I lift my head above the parapet,' Richard admitted. Yet Richard is a big believer in sharing knowledge and understands that the tech industry needs well-educated people. So he continues to contribute using his expertise and, in doing so, provides ethical and more accessible approaches and offerings that level the playing field and enhance opportunities for smaller businesses.

Mark Hayes refers to his inner critic as a 'frenemy': 'It's there alongside me and, while it can be a pain in the ass, it's not something I want to get rid of. Instead, I work with it – it drives me and stops me from being complacent. Its fire also helps me make the things I am doing better.'

Thought leadership is a constructive and productive way to challenge the status quo. Suzi, Richard, Mark, the Lifewise team, and countless other thought leaders genuinely and generously want to use what they know to help others. Their sense of purpose overcomes their reluctance. It still coexists with doubts, but – at least, at times – their sense of purpose calls more loudly. Your purpose will be the propellant that launches you forward. Its power is enough to make you want to move – as it has them. After all, if we're too comfortable, there's no need to go anywhere.

So far:

It can be exceptionally difficult to see the value of the work you're doing or the thoughts and ideas you have. Evidence points to the fact that it can be nearly impossible to have an accurate gauge on your own work.

So, while it might appear that others don't worry about whether they have enough value to offer, everyone does. When you are playing bigger and pushing for better, it's overwhelmingly common to feel resistance and reluctance. That does not mean that you need to stay stuck.

There are four aspects that provide a solid foundation from which to overcome your reluctance:

1. Look objectively at what you are doing to get an evidence-based view of the value you can contribute.
2. Value your experience, and loosen the hold that labels have by placing more importance on action and outcomes than arbitrary badges.
3. Accept that a negative internal voice is unavoidable, and invite it along for the ride.
4. Care enough to do it anyway. Find your fire for the thing that is still worth doing even though you are scared.

CHAPTER 4

What do we actually mean by authentic?

We were most of the way through our monthly marketing strategy check-in. We'd looked at how the website was performing, revisited the work-in-progress, and were tracking our movement towards the goals we had set when our consultant, Nathan Frater (or Nate to his friends), said, 'I think we should film some short marketing videos.' Half paying attention, while also jotting down the action point that we'd just finished discussing into my notebook, I nodded and said, 'Yep, cool, Verity can do that.'

Nate took a breath and looked directly at me. 'No,' he said, pausing to gauge that I was definitely listening. 'You both need to appear in the videos.'

I tried arguing. 'I really don't think that's a good idea,' I deflected. 'Verity usually does that stuff – she can be in them. That'll be fine.'

Nate wasn't having a bar of it. 'You both need to be in

these videos,' he explained. 'Some of them solo and a few together. You will appeal to different people.' I recall thinking what a strange comment that was. I couldn't see enough of a difference. We were both alike enough: white, young (millennial) women, both more-or-less brunette. But I trusted Nate, so I reluctantly agreed to what he was suggesting. From there, I zoned out for the rest of the meeting – disengaging as a form of protection and perhaps denial as Verity and Nate set out the next steps to make the videos happen. I was there in body, but far from present.

The day for recording rolled around (too quickly), and our normally welcoming and cosy meeting room was transformed. Cables snaked across the dark grey carpet. Nate's videographer set up two large rectangular lights that towered over the couches, pointing at what I figured would be the hot seat.

Verity and I had divided up the topics we were each going to talk about; she gave me first pick of the ones I'd feel more comfortable covering. I'd written talking points, and had read and reread them. I'd had my hair and makeup done and was as prepared as I could be, yet I still felt totally ill-equipped for the task at hand.

I bumbled through the first couple of takes, everyone doing what they could to smooth the way for me. Speaking to Nate off-camera, interview-style helped; I almost forgot the camera was there if I didn't have to look at it directly. 'Let's just have a conversation,' he soothed, amid assurances that it could all be fixed in editing later. Two painstaking hours later, Nate was satisfied. I had no idea how what I'd done had come across, when we wrapped up the day. I was just relieved it was over for now. Exhausted, I shuffled papers around my desk before packing up early and driving home.

I largely forgot about the filming – until the Dropbox folder link arrived in our inboxes, that is. I did not have high hopes for seeing how the clips had come together. Craning my head around our large desktop computer screens I could see that Verity was still engaged in another task so I had a moment to review them privately. I wanted to put it off, but couldn't resist knowing what they'd ended up like. Unable to remember which ones I would see myself on and which ones had been Verity's topics, I pressed play.

The first video I saw was one of Verity's. She was talking fast, at ease – and, although aiming her words at Nate off-screen, she looked directly at the camera, too. Her eye-contact was engaging. Her hands moved naturally to match her energy and underscore her confidence. She came across well – as I knew she would.

I scrolled down to another video – one relating to books – that I was sure was mine, and covered my eyes, peeking through my fingers as the image of my face filled the screen. The video began to play, and I didn't hate it. That was the first surprise. My second thought was that I was slow. Where Verity was leaning forward, talking in a constant stream and filling the space with her words and enthusiasm, I was obviously thinking as I spoke. My words came more slowly, and I could almost see the wheels turning in my head as I thought through my answers. I was sitting much further back in the seat and I look relaxed, almost nonchalant, but it was more a case of wishing the chair might swallow me up. The incredibly stark contrast between Verity's and my videos was apparent. But again, I didn't hate mine. What I was saying had value and, despite or perhaps because of my cadence, I came across as reserved yet thoughtful.

Seeing how vastly different – but still okay – these videos were was a huge turning point for me. I realised that I didn't need to be like Verity to be successful on video. I didn't need to be more confident, more adept at presenting, or a faster or louder talker; I could show up as me and still be effective. This might seem like an obvious realisation (and one that shouldn't have taken me 30-something years to discover), but it was game-changing for me. I had always hoped that the quiet and considered could have a voice, but had believed that surely for that to happen they would need to become more extroverted. Anything else, I feared, was me once again being idealistic. Yet here I was showing up as me, and the videos were well-received. Nate had been right; we appealed to different people. But I was right. too. I now had proof, however small, of what I had been hoping. It was the starting seed of belief that any of us could have an effective voice, without needing to change ourselves to become more like the others we see out there already having an impact. We could show up authentically and do things in a way that aligned with how we are.

•••

There is far more than just one way to be effective as a thought leader.

A significant thrust for me in writing this book is that I firmly believe that we need to widen the scope for what thought leadership can look like, and make room for different people to be effective with it. As we've seen throughout this journey already, there is a pernicious idea that there's a right way to come across in order to influence others – and that is, generally, as the larger-than-life sage on the stage. There's no doubt that this archetype is effective. That's why it has endured this long and maintained its foothold as our dominant model. The problem is that the rest of us haven't had much of a look-in. If I believe that I need to show up and present like Verity – whether in conversations or on video – then I will invariably fall short, simply because I am not Verity. She has her way, and I need my own.

Comparison is the thief of joy: it's guaranteed to make us feel inadequate, or feel that we are so far behind the mark that we may as well not even try. I had taken that position for too long, and I see it happening with too many of the other clever and generous people I know as well. Instead, we all need to find our own authentic brand of thought leadership, or form of magic. While there's no doubt that slick marketing can be convincing, and that performative shows work well to connect with audiences, you don't have to bend yourself to fit that mould. Your authentic, self-aligned brand of thought leadership will allow you to show up in a sustainable and empowered way, which is what will enable you to stay the course on the journey to becoming a thought leader who has lasting impact.

The dominant model has its merits

We know where the dominant model of thought leadership has come from. In the pursuit of greater influence, people who are doing great work have looked to those with the power to persuade, and modelled their activity from there. We've got an amalgamation of traits and tactics that define our prominent politicians and public figures, and this comprises now what we assume thought leaders should aspire to. And it *is* an assumption. When we consider these qualities on merit alone, they often don't stack up. We've seen that confidence doesn't necessarily confirm, or sometimes even overlap with, competence. That slickness is not necessarily equated with substance.

When people speak powerfully, decisively and with conviction, we can't argue its effectiveness, however. Verity brings a bold and convincing energy to her presentations and her conversations (years of stage performances for musical theatre and practice in debating have seen to that). She's able to distil things down to the key point or points easily, and is skilled at making those main messages sound good, too. Then her open delivery – with shoulders back, chest open, head held high, plentiful eye-contact and hands gesticulating to underscore each point – further cements what she's saying and increases the likelihood that we trust and believe her. There's nothing at all wrong with Verity's high-dose confidence; she's a highly skilled presenter, and a joy to watch. And when Verity admitted, in Chapter 1, that she tended to be able to do what she wanted to do more often, she was noticing the reality that – much more often than not – she's able to effectively convince others of her point of view.

However, we know that this way of showing up doesn't fit everyone (me included). Verity is confident coming across like that, as this reflects her natural and comfortable style. For the rest of us, it would take incredible acting skills to emulate this style and be even halfway convincing. Playing a part doesn't work. We all come across differently – a truth Nate noticed long before I did. Yet it's possible to put ourselves and our ideas out there in our own ways and make a positive difference for our clients and others around us. Despite how it can look at first glance, there's a broad amount of room for success. In order to be able to lead with our ideas and increase our impact in an effective way – and with genuine confidence on our side – we need to be bringing our unique version of thought leadership – and using our various strengths to contribute value.

Your authentic brand of thought leadership

In the same way that we saw how leadership has swung towards a celebration of authenticity, that same embracing of authenticity is what we need to see in thought leadership. Authentic leadership theory as a focused area of study may have emerged more recently, but ancient Greek philosophers were stressing the importance of authenticity centuries ago with refrains such as "Know thyself", emphasising that one should be in control of one's own life, act on one's own authority, or follow a moral inner voice.[47] In more modern times, we understand authenticity to be about acting in alignment with our values and desires, and showing up as who we really are without hiding. It's about acting in accordance with what we truly think and feel, and saying what we truly mean. It involves being true to ourselves, self-aware when it comes to our strengths, and vulnerable about sharing our shortcomings. The theory is that if leaders show up in this way in a work setting, they create an environment where other people feel safe to do so also.

Yet authenticity isn't only a buzzword for work or leadership. The case for being authentic in all avenues of our lives is compelling. Research shows that authentic people instil a sense of trust and earn our respect.[48] Whether in the public domain, our personal lives or professional settings, we admire people who have the courage to unapologetically be who they are. And we value integrity. Those who do what they say they're going to do, while being honest and acting with conviction, earn a unique respect. Perhaps unsurprisingly, people who are living more authentically experience enhanced happiness and greater wellbeing.[49] They are also more likely to experience higher self-esteem, and have stronger or more connected relationships with others. Although authenticity is something that is practised by us, it's something that is perceived and experienced by others. The people around us are generally well able to feel when someone is being genuine and authentic or conversely when they are trying to be someone or something that they are not. Where authenticity is present in our relationships and interactions, there is better communication, higher trust and psychological safety, and greater loyalty and engagement.

Just as there are different ways of leading that are effective, and just as there are many different thoughts about even the same topic that are valuable, so it is with thought leadership. Yes, thought leadership is something that you do, but the most authentic forms of it also celebrate who people are. There's a unique frequency that each one of us has that is our authentic thought leadership, and that's what we want to move towards. You don't need to talk to the frequency of everybody – in fact, trying to do so is likely to result in noise. Instead, you want to speak in your own unique frequency that will appeal to the people who need to hear what you're sharing. Just like different parts in a melody will appeal to different people, so too will your magic when it is shared in your own authentic way. Not only that, but authenticity is also what others are looking for: 90 percent of consumers report that they look for authenticity when deciding which brands to support.[50] It's happening with the choices we make with our wallets, and in matters of the heart, too: research has found that perceiving those who we are in a relationship with as authentic is correlated with higher interpersonal trust, relationship satisfaction and commitment.[51] We can sense when someone is showing up authentically and when they're not, and we connect with what's real. Similarly, we can see when people are trying to be like others because they think that's the formula for success. A cookie-cutter approach creates consistent cookie-cutter outcomes. It's simply repackaging, and it's a problem when it comes to the world of ideas. We've seen already that we don't want just one type of thought leadership or one type of thinking – that we need more diversity than that. Nothing is as good as the real or the original.

The challenges with authenticity

While in no way detracting from the basic truth of what has just been said, presenting authentically does need to be dished up with a side-serve of reality. A commitment to authenticity sounds all well and good, but the decision to show up as our most honest and real selves in any situation isn't always clear cut, even despite the many known benefits. In practice, the well-meaning advice to "just be authentic" or "just be yourself" comes with issues and pitfalls. For me, it sits somewhere alongside the tricky idea of "bringing our whole selves to work". Useful, but only to a point.

While there is undoubtedly value to anything that encourages more humanity, vulnerability and realness in our workplaces, I still can't help but think there are surely some parts of myself that deserve no place at work at all. The lazy part that wants to escape everyone, blob out and eat chocolate, as an example. There's also a part of me that's a lot less rational and a whole lot more reactive when I am on edge. Short of helping me better empathise with others and their array of emotions, those parts of me are not so useful or constructive in my work. So the advice to bring our whole selves to work comes with a few caveats. Namely: *in-so-far as we're being appropriate*. The same goes for the advice to be authentic. It's well-meaning and lovely in theory, but on some level we all know that there are some versions of authenticity that feel more appropriate, or better fit the brief, in each situation.

Michael Bungay Stanier, founder of Box of Crayons, summed this up well when he reflected on his promotional activity following the release of his book *How to Work With (Almost) Anyone*. Stanier was invited onto internet celebrity Lewis Howes' podcast, *The School of Greatness*, and confessed that, leading up to the interview, he was excited but nervous. This was only amplified by encountering Simon Sinek walking out of his interview as Stanier walked in. No stranger to proactively harnessing curiosity, however, Stanier decided to ask Lewis and his team – before they got started with the interview – what made the difference between a great interviewee and just another good one. They all said that it came down to being authentic. Stanier shares that this advice was tricky for him to navigate and didn't really tell him anything practical because he was well aware that 'authentic him' is 'often taciturn, slightly grumpy, and watching Netflix in Toronto, not shiny and entertaining in a studio in L.A.'[52] Stanier felt pretty sure they wanted the latter, not the former though, and I think you'd agree. On some level, we intuitively know that there's still a *version* of the "real us" that is going to be appropriate or effective in a given situation. We instinctively know that there's a type that's more helpful in certain domains: a version of authentic that each occasion demands. (Just as there is a "wholeness of self" that work demands, and a little bit that work would rather request you leave at home to deal with later.) In the same way that it can be challenging to get an accurate gauge on the value we're bringing to the world through our work, it can also be challenging to understand the context, and trust that we can show up authentically, to be successful.

We face myriad pressures to conform in almost any given situation, and many of us make assumptions about the attitudes, beliefs, and sometimes even the paths of our peers, while downplaying what we most want or feel. Sometimes sticking to what you know or feel to be right means going against the crowd, which is difficult. We prize fitting in, as Dr Bex Bell's work, described in the last chapter, attests. We also constantly take cues about what's effective and appropriate based on what is happening around us, what is valued or prized in our society, and what looks like it's working. We form stories around this, that we then treat as fact. Yet none of it is immutable. We've seen this in action already in the dominant ideas of what types of people are successful in Susan Cain's 'extroverted ideal'. It's easy to accept those ideas as some kind of universal law because they appear to be so widely and commonly-accepted across the various domains in our lives.

If we lift our heads out of the system we're operating in, we start to see that even those ideas are not absolutes. In non-Western cultures, very different traits are valued. With a broad brush, Cain highlights those typifying what she refers to as 'soft power'. Where Western culture broadly values boldness, verbal skill and individuality, Cain notes, Asian cultures revere quiet, humility and sensitivity, which together foster group cohesion.[53] I have had to let go of some of my beliefs about certain traits as I have been doing this work, too. I'd always thought, for example, that humility was a good and desirable thing, and that we should be modest, gracious and never boastful. However, too much of even something that we think is good can prove unhelpful. An overabundance of humility can get in the way of your ability to serve others, for example.

No traits are either all good or all bad, but each have a "right-size" that is helpful and healthy, and that depends on each individual and on the specific situation or context. Everything is conditional. Yet, if we're unable to loosen our grip on the stories we're subject to, or at least consider that they are not absolutes or whole truths, we'll stay stuck and trapped. We'll fail to see other alternatives, and will further perpetuate the dominant archetype that exists, allowing it to keep its current power.

We need people actively proving what's possible, opening up the space around what's successful, and allowing greater possibilities. So many of the reluctant thought leaders that I talk to apologetically feel they need to ask permission to deviate in any way from the dominant picture of what seems like it's working. I don't believe they need permission, but I readily dole out reassurance and provide a friendly nudge that I'm now extending to you, too.

We're going to look more at adaptability and authentic thought leadership shortly – but there's one final caveat to make about authenticity.

Authenticity doesn't allow us to "phone it in"

It's tempting to think that being authentic doesn't require a lot from us; that it offers us the path of least resistance. Surely, if we just have to be ourselves, then that's easy, right? We all already know how to do that. We've had many years of practice. To some extent, this is true and a positive thing. We also know we're going to need to bring some energy to what we're doing in order to succeed and have an incredible impact, even if we are acting authentically. In sharing the video of his podcast interview with Howes, Stanier quips that we will see him doing his best to be animated, funny, wise, vulnerable, encouraging and entertaining. He also goes on to admit that this doesn't just happen, but took practice, planning and intention.

Just showing up as ourselves isn't always successful. If it were, then all of us who were quietly going about our lives and being ourselves in the meantime would be achieving everything we hoped for. That's simply not the case.

Our authentic thought leadership is going to see us less guarded, working to our purpose, enjoying what we do, and fulfilling more of our potential. But it's also not the easy road. We need the right balance of challenge and comfort. You will absolutely start by operating in the ways that are most aligned to you, but you won't stop there. Some resistance is healthy, and helps us push to explore new parts of our personalities, learn new skills, and succeed beyond what we previously thought possible. We'll look more at how we get that balance right in Chapter 9.

Adapting for authenticity

Adapting and being authentic may seem contradictory. Where the former implies that we modify or adjust to different conditions or purposes, the latter implies that we are, to some extent, steadfast and unwavering in our assured selves.

Every day, and in multiple ways, we adapt to our surroundings. We soften our voices when we are giving feedback or want to make a request in a more polite way. We force ourselves to speak up, even if that's not what we're usually like in meetings, if someone is being treated unfairly, or if we really feel that we need our opinion or input to be heard. We might tone down our swearing if we are spending time with our grandparents or perhaps visiting a church, to signal respect. In these and countless other ways, we conduct ourselves differently at different times, based on context and what we are wanting to convey and achieve. Being effectively or successfully authentic includes a delicate balance between being who you truly are and expressing how you really feel, while still showing up in the way that's best for the situation: appropriate and accepted. This isn't inauthentic. It's smart, and it's what is required to be effective.

Again, the world of leadership theory provides a precedent. The Situational Leadership Model was first created by behavioural scientist Dr Paul Hersey and leadership expert Dr Ken Blanchard while working on the widely used 1996 textbook, *Management of Organizational Behavior*. Situational theories of leadership work on the assumption that no single leadership style is better than another but, instead, the most effective style of leadership changes from situation to situation. As Suzi McAlpine attests, the best leaders are intentional about what leadership approach is called for *in each moment*, and then adapt their style to what's required.[54] She agrees that this doesn't signal a lack of authenticity. Rather, as she puts it, situational leadership is a bit like having a toolkit with different hammers for different nails. Successfully practicing situational leadership requires understanding that there's no one-size-fits-all model for leading a team, and that different situations demand different responses, as do different people. Effective leaders can read the situation or context within their organisation and adapt to provide what that situation calls for. As a leader, the ability to adapt is a superpower.

Thought leadership is no different. Being successful or effective depends not on the acquisition of prescriptive traits that are better than others, nor even a fixed way of being you, but on finding an authentic way to get results in a given situation. And luckily, there are many ways to be effective.

I like to think of it like a mixing desk – the kind that's used to balance music when you are recording or playing live. To those unfamiliar with one of these set-ups, it's a large console with what looks like an infinite number of sliding knobs and dials. There are dials for controlling everything from the bass to the drums to any other instrument that you have plugged in. For simplicity's sake, let's just look at one of its functions: adjusting the volume of each of the inputs. Turning everything right down means there's no music, and no magic. When we turn everything up, we get full volume, and a lot of nasty noise. If one or two instruments are far too dominant in the mix, they drown everything else out, and make it impossible to hear what is truly being said in the music. Yet it's not a case of set and forget; the same instruments don't have to be equal across the entire song, either. Variety is important. The same thing goes for us. We all have this beautiful bundle of strengths and traits that we can arrange into a harmonious symphony. This is why I feel so strongly about redrawing the rules and opening up what thought leadership can be, to make it more accessible to everyone.

A better version of thought leadership encourages the use of more people's unique gifts, which hold so much value. Doing nothing means we make no contribution, and trying to do it *all* likely equates to a mess. The key is balance: both authenticity and adaptability are hugely important to our new and broader iterations of thought leadership. It's easy to think that some of our traits confirm that we're not great candidates for thought leadership. It might be more accurate to say that we are over- or under-playing them. It could be the level they are coming through at, not their existence at all, that's causing the noise. Following this logic, you no longer need to worry that you are not *X-enough*, or *good-at-X-enough*, to have a bigger impact. It's true that you might not have every instrument in the orchestra, but you most assuredly have combinations that can make a perfectly serviceable sound. A workable combination that enables you to contribute something positive and worthwhile.

Daria Williamson, the strengths coach we first encountered in Chapter 3, uses the analogy of a house to explain the versatility of our strengths and traits and the way that we can work with them. Say the outcome you needed was to share a fantastic idea you had with your team, and then win them over to your way of thinking. In this instance, the *Centre Stage* strength (defined as the ability to engage others' attention, speak up in groups and naturally hold the floor) might be considered the metaphorical key to the front door. It would be the exact or most obvious strength that you need in that situation in order to be effective. However, say you didn't have *Centre Stage* in your toolkit. That doesn't mean that the outcome of persuading others and winning them over to your ideas is simply not available to you. There's never just one way to achieve what you're working towards. You may need to find a different – an authentically "you" way – to achieve the same outcome. Another way into the house, so to speak. You might instead be able to draw on something like the *Storyteller* strength (your ability to weave engaging stories to share insights, lessons, values and humour), or *Rapport Builder* (the ability to make positive connections with new people and win them over), coupled with your natural empathy. In our analogy, this might be akin to going in the side door or through a window, but that's totally okay if it gets you in the house.

In theory, we can do anything if we put our mind to it and invest enough time and energy in pursuit of that outcome. But that doesn't mean that we should, or that it's a good use of our resources. Acting a part that isn't real for you doesn't work. It's akin to trying to chisel or tunnel your way into the house using a teaspoon. Again, you might get there eventually, but it's very unlikely to have been worth the effort. It will require an outsized amount of energy to get anywhere close to an outcome. As with most things in life, the best path is never going to be in trying to be something that you are not.

Nor should you be subverting other qualities that make you great in order to fit the mould.

This isn't only a nice ideal, but it's also a practical necessity. The pursuit of real impact has a slow burn. You have to show up, again and again, in service of your ideas and the people you are here to make an impact for and with. This means that the things you do need to have a long shelf-life. You have to engage in activity that's sustainable for the long-term. You might be able to rally to do something that's really not aligned to you and your natural style as a one-off, as I could on that day of filming our first batch of marketing videos. Do that every day, though, and you will soon find yourself burning out. We can't maintain the motivation or the energy for things that don't feel good, or that push us too far away from ourselves. We're far better to work from the strengths that we do have and weave together a composite that works. Real and authentic thought leadership allows you to show up continuously because you're not abusing yourself in order to fit.

A great sense of power comes from acting according to your strengths. Acting in an aligned way – one that feels natural and, at least to some degree, comfortable to you – takes far less energy than acting the part. Not only does it allow others to better trust and connect with what you are sharing, but you're also better able to sustain what you're there to do. You waste energy when you try to act like something you're not, when you under-value your own talents, and when you allow yourself to be underestimated by others. You know you're going to have to push beyond your most comfortable state if you hope to have huge impact, but starting from a place of comfort gives you a strong foundation – one from which it's possible to find flow and experience boundless energy.

Cain shares an example of this in action – that of an introverted Wall Street lawyer. (Readers later learn the lawyer in this story is actually Cain.) Having made it through Harvard Law School, she worried that she could not represent her clients as forcefully as they may have expected. Working initially as a junior, it was years until she had to test this assumption. One day though, her senior partner went on holiday, leaving her in charge of an important negotiation. Fighting her impulse to hide under the table, she sat quietly and listened to the lawyer on the other side deliver her speech, all the while picturing the bold, smooth, table-pounding person who she thought would be better placed than she herself was to save the day in this particular situation. She was a long way out of her comfort zone and promised herself that she'd make it through that meeting, then look for a different career. Then she remembered what she'd been learning: that because she was an introvert, she had unique powers in negotiation. These powers might be less obvious at first glance, but could be no less formidable. As Cain shares,

> She'd probably prepared more than everyone else. She had a quiet but firm speaking style. She rarely spoke without thinking. Being mild-mannered, she could take strong, even aggressive positions, while coming across as perfectly reasonable. And she tended to ask questions – lots of them – and actually listen to the answers, which, no matter what your personality, is crucial to strong negotiation.[55]

She took a deep breath and started to do what came naturally to her: stepping back, relooking at the numbers, and asking lots of questions. She stayed true to her own style, and the mood in the room changed. The posturing and dominating simmered down and they started to have a real conversation, finally striking a deal. She got the outcome and she'd done it her way.

That's the music we're aiming for – the type that enables us to right the balance, welcome more potential contributors in, and see more of the good ideas out in the world. Rewriting the rules of thought leadership allows us to embrace the benefits of our differences and achieve what we're capable of – all while strengthening our collective ideascape and moving us towards better outcomes, solutions and ideas.

You have powers that, while perhaps less obvious at first glance, can be no less formidable when it comes to thought leadership. I've mentioned a few times the idea of finding a combination or composite that works. What we need is the broad rules – the box that we are playing within in order to succeed with thought leadership – so that we can bring what we've got to that.

Finding a combination that works

We know that we need thought leadership, and that we want it to be better, broader and more inclusive – in both its thinking and its leading elements. So how do we now get there? If we were to throw out the existing rulebook, and instead imagine what the best kind of thought leadership would look like for the world we are living in and the challenges we're facing, what would you come up with?

For me, the best thought leaders have incredible ideas,

great frameworks, and game-changing ways of doing things. They also have a genuine and generous desire to help more people. They are purpose-driven, fuelled by conviction and a clear vision of better that they are taking us towards. They're humble, inclusive and empathetic. They're open to learning and gathering more perspectives. They're committed to proactively improving and developing what they know. They're curious and considered, bringing robust thought and deep reasoning to the challenges they are solving. And they're backed by extensive experience, meaning they don't just have a collection of wild theories, but have lived out, tested and proven their ideas. They've collected the evidence that shows that what they are thinking works.

That might seem like a lot, or like I have simply created a new set of prescriptive boxes to tick, but it's much less about what a thought leader is or has, and more about what they are doing to successfully achieve a positive impact and contribute value to the world.

In terms of thinking, we need ideas that push our boundaries and open us up to new possibilities. We need ideas that aren't necessarily the promise of a "sure thing", ideas that might still be experimental, and that are backed by experience. We need ideas that consider a range of angles and perspectives, and that contain nuance and allow for complexity. We need to see more ideas that aren't claiming to be the finish-line or the full truth, but are still a work-in-progress, ones that aren't yet fully formed, but that contain seeds that propel us forward. And, we need ideas that not only allow for, but invite, continual learning and evolution. This is the thinking that both comes from and encourages active, informed and respectful debate.

In terms of leading, we don't just want to hear from those who we are historically used to hearing from. We need voices and ideas that represent varied perspectives. To get this, we need to encourage, hold up, and celebrate all the types of people who are bringing forward into the world thinking that makes us better. We need to encourage different ways of taking and sharing our ideas, and different ways of inspiring and motivating action. This means different terms of engagement. What works for the quiet and the considered types – the thinkers – is necessarily and vastly different to what works for the talkers. We don't want everyone to be playing the same game, which is why we are rewriting the playbook.

A better and broader path for thought leadership:

- invites and embraces complexity,
- acknowledges uncertainty,
- is non-threatening, inclusive and collaborative, and
- is never fixed but instead constantly evolves and improves.

Four qualities for BETTER

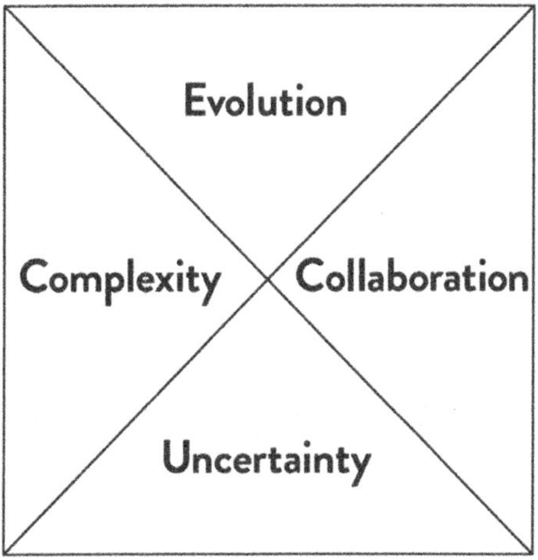

In the chapters that follow, we will dive deeper into why each of these four aspects is so vital in a better and broader iteration of thought leadership – and how these qualities encourage better thinking, ideas, outcomes and, ultimately, impact.

Part Two

CHAPTER 5

When complexity is a good thing

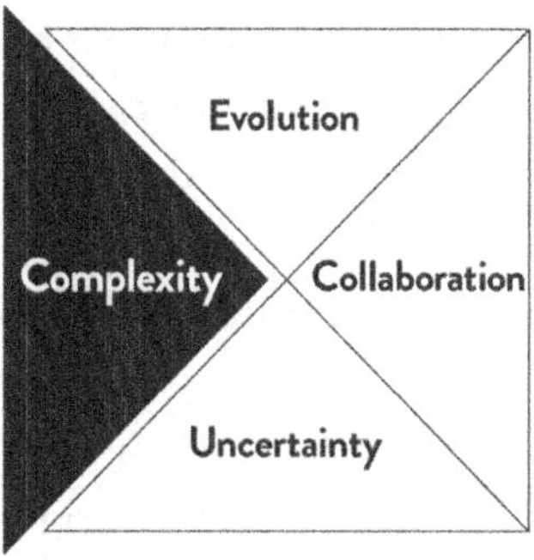

Look back at the 20th century, and you'll find few figures as well-admired as Winston Churchill. A giant in his time, Churchill has come to represent courage and resolute leadership during the Second World War. His tenacity and unwavering determination in the face of adversity was a testament to profound resilience and proved instrumental in shaping the course of history. A superlative statesman, and a diplomat who fought for democracy, Churchill provided a beacon of hope during the United Kingdom's darkest hours. His eloquent speeches, like the famous 'We shall fight on the beaches' address, continue to echo through the corridors of history, and rightly so.

But dig deeper, and a more complex picture of the man emerges, including some difficult truths that rarely appear in fawning biopics, nationalistic newspaper articles, or high-school history curriculums. For example, his views on race and imperialism are difficult to reconcile today. As John Charmley notes in *Churchill: The End of Glory*, Churchill believed in racial hierarchies and eugenics. In his testimony to the Palestine Royal Commission in 1937, Churchill said that 'no great wrong' had been done to the first peoples of North America (he used the term 'Red Indians') or Australia ('black people'): 'I do not admit that a wrong has been done to these people by the fact that a stronger race, a higher-grade race, a more worldly wise race to put it that way, has come in and taken their place.'[56] Read that and, like me, you'd probably wince. It certainly would be career suicide for a politician to say this today.

Churchill was a product of his time, many would argue. His views were quite mainstream for his era, that much is true. And he also is quoted as uttering some rather progressive statements, such as 'We will endeavour as far as we can to advance the principle of equal rights of civilised men irrespective of colour,' in 1906.[57] But these and other statements must be taken together, if we are to build up a complete picture of this figure. He was anti-union, and, in his early days, rejected women's right to vote 'on the grounds that it is contrary to natural law and the practice of civilized states[;] that no necessity is shown[;] that only the most undesirable class of women are eager for the right[; and] that those women who discharge their duty to the state viz marrying and giving birth to children are adequately represented by their husbands ….'[58]

Let's also not forget that, as First Lord of the Admiralty in the First World War, Churchill was largely responsible for the disasterous invasion of Gallipoli, and demoted as a consequence – something that makes his rehabilitation, selection and success as a wartime leader for the Second World War all the more remarkable.

Some of Churchill's views and history may be new, or confronting to you, as they were to me. And that's okay. Knowing these things about a person doesn't make their deeds any the less great, but it does temper our image of them. Churchill did great deeds in his lifetime and as a leader, yet who he was as a person, his experience, and the beliefs he held reflect a far more complicated picture.

•••

If we are brave enough to dig below the surface of an idea or an identity, we may end up with some complicated feelings. That is the price of seeing the bigger picture. Conversely, we lose something when we simplify thinking down to within an inch of its life. We lose the nuance, the light and shade. To simplify something, we necessarily reduce it to consider only one or two aspects, as is true when we zero in on Churchill as the infallible hero of the Second World War. Other details or factors no longer fit, so we discard them to suit our needs. The image becomes one-dimensional, but the ramifications stretch further.

Consider, by way of a different example, the leading economic indicator that's become our principal means of judging how our economies and societies are progressing: gross domestic product (GDP). In modern times, economic health has become a proxy for a country's wellbeing, but this doesn't take into account rising inequality, global imbalances, or other factors that have a significant impact on wellbeing. From an economic perspective, the world largely keeps getting better, so that should be a recipe for happiness. Yet many of us could point to other statistics and experiences that suggest that this is simply not the case. What we're measuring, and patting ourselves on the back for, is purely growth in production and consumption, and there's far more to it than that. David Pilling, author of *The Growth Delusion*, explains the problem:

> If the experts have designed a system that does not help us understand our reality, then the government is also left without a reliable metric with which to understand society. And if what we are measuring is wrong, or insufficient, then what we get, in terms of direction and policy, will be wrong and insufficient too. Governments make policies to maximise measured outcomes. For decades that has meant maximizing growth.[59]

As is evident in both of these examples, when we accept and project only the simplest solution or information, we lose some of the picture and, often, at least some of the truth.

Sometimes this is okay. Think about stripping back your wardrobe to retain just a number of the same or similar black t-shirts that you pair with pants. Now you've cut down the number of choices that you must make daily – reducing the "decision fatigue" that comes as a result of having to make too many micro-choices. You're keeping more of your cognitive capacity free for the tasks or decisions that truly matter, the ones that really do need your mental energy. This is useful and smart. Richard Branson, Mark Zuckerberg and Barack Obama subscribe to a minimalist closet for this reason.[60] The same principle can be applied to weekday dinner options: strip the menu back to a few crowd-pleasers, and it makes the choice easier, while keeping the chances high that everyone will be content with the evening meal. The distinction here and the reason this works, however, is that the stakes are relatively low when it comes to what we eat and what we're wearing.

The same does not apply in the world of ideas or when we're influencing others' thinking. Here we strip too much out to everyone's detriment. In many cases, we can't afford to lose part of the picture or the truth, or to miss out on understanding the underlying reasoning and justification. It's dangerous when simple information is put forward not only as fact, but also as the full story. When it comes to ideas, simplification can easily go too far.

Philosophers have long been aware of the "reductive fallacy of oversimplification" that can lead to flaws in reasoning, invalid arguments and intentional misdirection. The root of this is what is known in psychology and cognitive science as schema: a kind of pattern of categorisation that has evolved to save us time and energy. As we learn about the world, we group concepts and mental images together and give them a kind of shorthand, so we don't have to look too closely or think too much. We expect horses to have four legs and manes; we expect sedans to all have a particular shape. We have mental frameworks for how we are supposed to behave on a first date, or act around our grandparents.[61] Schema are also the root of stereotypes, both positive and negative, and, as much as they can be helpful, they can be harmful and extremely limiting, too. Categories ultimately blur out important details; they're efficient, yet slippery.

When we attempt to make something appear simpler, we too often ignore relevant complexities. So a world, or a collective ideascape, built solely on oversimplified stories becomes a tenuous one. We see this in our tendency to assume a single or simple cause for an outcome, when that outcome was, in reality, caused by a number of contributing factors. Simply concluding that smoking alone caused someone's cancer, or that video-game use is to blame for increasing violence, ignores additional or inter-connected reasons and shuts our minds down to other possibilities. As a result, any solutions we then try are only going to be mildly effective, at best. Again, we're seeing only part of the picture, and that's far from the full truth.

Simplification isn't solely our fault

To some extent, oversimplification is not our fault, and nor is it always intentional. Sometimes simplification is necessary for us to be able to understand our complex world.

We've all experienced the increased quantity and speed of information coming at us. Our brains have a lot to do, so it's both understandable and practical that they create mental shortcuts. Simple rules allow us to react quickly to emergency situations – for example, in those contexts where we need split-second judgements and actions. Simplification can save lives here.

Other times we need to ignore certain factors initially in order to get our heads around something difficult. In this case, oversimplifying complex challenges can make them seem less daunting. Breaking a challenge into its respective components can help us feel as though we have greater command over the issue at hand.

Simplification can also obscure critical interdependencies and lead to a false sense of security, as can happen when you draw analogies from challenges that you've faced in the past. Starting from a simple strategy, or a tried-and-true technique can be useful because it gives you somewhere to work from, but it can also lead you to miss the unique nuances of the present issue. Unsurprisingly, problems arise if we hold tight to our simplified view, aren't willing to budge with new information or evidence, or willingly stay ignorant. We miss things that could help us to relate better to the people around us, come up with better solutions, or enhance our expertise.

Alongside our brains' tendencies when they're struggling with too much complexity, we're also juggling multiple devices simultaneously, while being constantly interrupted by pinging notifications and increasing competition for our attention. Just as cultural conditions created the dominant model of thought leadership, they're also pushing us down the road to oversimplification. In the race to gain and keep our attention, we've seen the rise of clickbait, stripped-out, sensationalised soundbites, and social media algorithms designed to favour particular (and, for the most part, perpetually shrinking) formats of information. Substance is lost here. It's difficult to present a balanced argument in 280 characters. And even when we consider content beyond a single tweet (or is it now a xeet?), best practice urges us to keep things clear and concise.

We're encouraged to avoid getting bogged down in too many details. Leonardo da Vinci may have said that simplicity is the ultimate sophistication, but it isn't always the better option.

Stopping the downward spiral of simplification

If we always choose the cognitively easier route, we're training ourselves to be less able, and less willing, to handle and accept nuance as we work to navigate complicated aspects of our world. In reality, most people have complex and ambivalent feelings about many things, as well as uneven knowledge and varying opinions. Yet many discussions force us to choose one of only two sides and see the world in just two dimensions.[62] The danger is that as we become accustomed to the push-button conveniences of modern life, we begin to crave that in all things.

Entrepreneur Chris Myers, writing about oversimplification for *Forbes*, believes that this is happening in our thinking, and that we're 'rapidly transforming into a society that is crass, shallow and often oblivious … increasingly ruled by laziness and emotion'.[63] This may be an easier path, but it is ultimately a fruitless one.

Commentators have raised concerns around Google's view of information as a kind of commodity, and the impact this is having on our brains in terms of sustained thought and attention. The aim of Google's game is for us to be able to process information with the utmost efficiency and get the gist of things as quickly as possible so that we'll keep clicking. It's not doing our brains any favours as we're overloaded with an influx of information. And, thanks to the plasticity of our brain's pathways, the more we use the internet, the more we train our brain to be distracted. As journalist Nicholas Carr describes it, we're learning 'to process information very quickly and very efficiently but without sustained attention.'[64]

And that's the more benign scenario; simplification can also be used to deliberately deceive and divide. In his article 'How Oversimplifying a Complex World Drives Us Apart', criminal defence attorney and writer Craig Blake asserts: 'We want heroes and villains, not complicated human beings. We want people to be "good" or "bad", not a muddled combination of both.'[65] We simplify them down to a single category. And we fall prey to this polarisation, even though we consciously know that no single person is actually solely all good or all bad. Everyone falls squarely into that "muddled combination" camp. Not only does simplification perpetuate incomplete or false characterisations of people, but it encourages us to become more prepared to accept simplified perceptions and misconceptions of other phenomena around us. In other words, it's not just people we are doing this with. Binary bias sees us processing all manner of information, especially contentious issues, in a simplified and dichotomous way as either good or bad, black or white. We tend to consider ideas as one of two possibilities, despite the fact that most issues are best considered on a continuum of information and perspectives.

As helpful as oversimplifying can be, it can also cause problems. When we ignore, obscure, or simply fail to take into account additional factors, we run a high risk of misunderstanding reality, and misunderstanding others. Addressing issues from a place of misunderstanding can never lead to comprehensive solutions or effective action.

Philosophers believe that oversimplification is a common and recurring problem that keeps us 'trapped in dead-end and counterproductive theories and perspectives which have taken us away from truth and understanding instead of toward them'.[66] At some point, our propensity for simplification veers into dangerous territory – and that's certainly the case when it comes to the collective conversations in which thought leadership plays a part. If we only engage with convenient, oversimplified thought processes, and view complexity as an enemy to be eliminated, then we aren't having enough of the complex conversations. We are failing to engage in the productive and honest discussions about issues that lack one simple answer. Yet, these are just the sorts of issues we need to address and work together to solve if we want to make things better for all of us.

A case for complex arguments

It's possible to stop the downward spiral of simplification. Admittedly, it requires effort, but that effort – when it's geared towards better outcomes and better thinking – is always worth it.

Having seen the shortcomings of GDP as a marker of a nation's success or vitality, much work has been done to broaden back out what we're measuring. Aotearoa New Zealand made headlines across the world for our move towards a "wellbeing budget" where wellbeing is a crucial marker influencing how priorities are set and resources allocated.[67] The World Wide Fund for Nature, the Wellbeing Economy Alliance, and the European Environmental Bureau have since joined forces to call for other economies to move beyond GDP as the measure of a society's progress and replace it with alternative metrics so that we see more of the resulting policies prioritise long-term societal and environmental goals around wellbeing, inclusion and sustainability.[68] This is a fantastic example of how nuance contributes to making sure we are well-balanced and better-understanding humans – and that we're putting forward more considered and effective solutions. But that's far from the only benefit of nuance. More nuanced or complex arguments can also be more compelling and convincing, despite not looking so at first glance.

This chapter will be especially encouraging to those reluctant thought leaders who also identify as over-thinkers and struggle to simplify what they do down into a spiffy soundbite. Those deep and reflective wonderers who are wary of oversimplified arguments, and avoid perpetuating more of the same. We need more of you to lead the charge – and put forward arguments that consider multiple angles and different perspectives.

Far from being a stumbling block, your struggle to strip your argument down so far might actually be a superpower, especially if you are tackling a topic or solving an issue that is multi-faceted and complex. Prolific author and pioneer of lateral thinking Dr Edward de Bono suggests that cleverness is a sharp-focus camera lens, while wisdom is a wide-angle lens.[69] In other words, we need to look beyond the simple and obvious of what's in front of us. We need to consider context, inter-relationships, and what's around the edges.

In *High Conflict: Why We Get Trapped and How We Get Out*, Amanda Ripley argues that the fundamental lesson for anyone who wants to cultivate healthy conflict is to complicate the narrative early – and often. She believes that pointing out variances encourages curiosity.

Similarly, in *Think Again,* author and Professor of Organisational Psychology Adam Grant encourages complexifying (his term for showcasing the full range of perspectives on a given topic) as an antidote for the oversimplified thinking tracks that land us in those binary binds. He attests that, while we might think that we're making progress when we discuss sensitive issues or complex challenges as two sides of the same coin, there are rarely only two perspectives. If we acknowledge the complexity that exists and present more issues as multi-layered, we can have a more considerable and more constructive impact.

Grant shares findings that have come from psychologist Peter T. Coleman's research at Columbia University's Difficult Conversations Lab. Those brave enough to visit the second-storey brick building are matched up with a stranger who strongly disagrees with their stance on a controversial topic. This isn't something many people willingly walk into, but we're lucky that hundreds have in support of science. Before your 20-minute slot to discuss the issue – after which you'll both decide whether you're aligned enough to sign a joint statement on your shared views – you're given an article about a different divisive topic to read. Think of it as a primer to get you into the right mindset. If you read an article that presents both sides of the issue and makes a balanced case, you have an increased chance of reaching consensus in the conversation that follows.

Impressive, but that was just the start of the experiment. Coleman then went on to create another version of the article for pre-reading that resulted in 100 percent of conversational partners reaching consensus. The alternative article included the same information as the other version, but presented the information differently. 'Instead of describing the issue as a black-and-white disagreement between two sides, the article framed the debate as a complex problem with many shades of gray, representing a number of different viewpoints,' Grant explains.[70] The results attest that people are more inclined to reconsider their views, accept alternative perspectives and think again, when topics are presented through the many lenses of a prism.

Other research backs this up. Researchers found that when journalists acknowledge the uncertainties around facts on complex issues – in other words, when they present a complex issue as being complex – it doesn't undermine their readers' trust.[71] Rather, doing this demonstrates that they are considering different viewpoints and presenting a balanced argument. As readers, we feel that no-one is trying to pull the wool over our eyes.

Similarly, other studies have shown that when experts express doubt – when they profess to not knowing the whole picture, because complex things are rarely completely knowable – they become more persuasive.[72] As Grant states: 'A dose of complexity can disrupt over-confidence cycles and spur rethinking cycles. It gives us more humility about our knowledge and more doubts about our opinions, and it can make us curious enough to discover information we were lacking.'[73] This is an excellent place to start, especially given that the leading part of thought leadership is about influencing and inspiring others.

Complex arguments encourage others to become curious, and rethink their own views. We need more of this. In showing up to build your thought leadership and increase your impact your way, we need you to advance arguments that consider multiple angles and portray different perspectives. You don't need to condense it all down to its lowest denominator. Bring us information that is inclusive and well-considered. The sorts of stories, examples and conversations that show us there is more to it than perhaps originally meets the eye.

So, how do we do this better?

Some of us may be naturally better at nuance. In *Quiet,* Susan Cain highlights the work of Jerome Kagan – to her mind one of the great developmental psychologists of the twentieth century – who devoted his career to studying the emotional and cognitive development of children. Kagan and his colleagues were able to identify 'high-reactive' and 'low-reactive' infants, as well as those who sat somewhere in-between, from as young as four months old. As you might imagine, the high-reactive group were those babies who cried heartily and wildly waved their arms and legs in response to new stimuli. The low-reactive group, on the other hand, stayed quiet and placid, despite balloons popping, new voices in the room, colourful mobiles dancing before their eyes, and strong smells being introduced into the space. The pairing of these descriptions and terms makes sense, however, the leap that Kagan made next was not so intuitive.

Kagan predicted that the infants in the high-reactive group were the ones more likely to grow into quiet or introverted teenagers, while those who stayed placid and quiet during the experiment would more likely be extroverted. This seems counter-intuitive, but his theory was correct. His in-depth longitudinal study found that the high-reactive infants were more likely to have developed serious, careful personalities as they grew older, while the quieter and less reactive infants were more likely to have grown up relaxed and confident. Measuring physiological reactions of the nervous system, like heart rates and blood pressure, helped to explain the link. These reactions are controlled by the amygdala – the emotional switchboard in the brain that receives information from the senses and signals us on how to respond. We all have different levels of sensitivity in our nervous system, which explains some important things about the way we show up in the world.

Those who are more prone to notice scary things – i.e. our high-reactive infants – are also more likely to notice things in general. They pay what one psychologist refers to as "alert attention" to people and things. In fact, research has shown they literally use more eye movements than others to compare choices before making a decision.[74] It's as if these people process the information they take in about the world more deeply. They think and feel in complex ways about what they are seeing, and they bring an extra degree of nuance to everyday experiences. These people are over-represented by those who would consider themselves to be introverts, and these quieter traits – alertness, sensitivity to nuance, and complex emotionality – have typically been under-rated.

A similar awareness of nuance is true for experts. When you have gone deep and enhanced your expertise, you will also notice more.[75] Wherever you fall on the introvert–extrovert spectrum, the pairing of passion for thought and attention to subtlety is a powerful combination. It's also a key driver for better thought leadership – encouraging the less polarising and divisive thinking, conversations and solutions that we so desperately need. It's further evidence, I believe, that our currently reluctant thought leaders have the power to change things for the better.

Many think that ideas are better if they can be spread wider and further, but not if their substance gets thinner and simpler. Powerful impact comes from making what you are doing stronger, deeper, fuller. Speaker and author Pete Davis likens it to building a powerful radio transmitter: 'It's rooted in one place, but if it's robust enough, its message will resonate further.'[76]

With practice, care and conscious effort, more complex arguments can be an option for everyone. It starts with harnessing an ability to identify and resist oversimplification, before challenging yourself to look beyond the obvious, then focusing your ideas into something workable, and finally finding a format for sharing your message most effectively.

Let's take a look at those four steps in more detail.

1. Identify and resist oversimplification

The first step, as with so many things, begins with awareness and a new perspective. We need to be able to spot oversimplification in the wild – both in information that we are consuming, and in the patterns of our own thinking. Then we need to welcome more complexity in. Recognising instances of oversimplification happening around us is relatively easily done when you start looking for it; we're surrounded by examples, and it's certainly easier to see oversimplification from a distance. Grant suggests that, as consumers of information, we have a role to play in embracing a more nuanced point of view. 'When we're reading, listening, or watching, we can learn to recognize complexity as a signal of credibility. We can favour content and sources that present many sides of an issue rather than just one or two.'[77]

Pinpointing instances of oversimplification in our own thinking is more challenging. We don't have that distance. Instead, it requires skill in what is referred to as "metacognition" – the process of intentionally thinking about our thinking and learning. It requires a great deal of self-awareness and a willingness to slow down and to engage in self-monitoring and evaluation. It's common for high-achievers to have a bias for action, so seeing where we might be oversimplifying, and stopping long enough to broaden out our views can feel painful. Instead of caving into the desire for a quick resolution, consciously balance your need for action with a more disciplined and deep-thinking approach to understanding the problem.

Look for simple, binary thoughts and statements that you make, and consider what additional perspectives might be missing between those two extremes. Recognise when you are quick to conclude that you're on the "good" or "right" side of an issue or argument, without exerting any effort or giving it any extra thought. This is a red flag that you need to dig deeper and allow for more complexity.

When you find yourself there, ask yourself:

- What am I inclined to believe about this topic? What would I like to be true?
- Can I uncover why or how this has come to be my most comfortable position?
- Why do I believe what I believe? What has informed my current understanding?
- What would it mean if the opposite were true?

This isn't about suddenly questioning everything that you

believe, or de-stabilising your mental foundation to the point where you feel like you are casting around in a cognitive wilderness. But it is about challenging yourself to identify when you have adopted a position a little too easily. This can provide clues that you may have arrived at something too simple or reductive, and where you could possibly do with a bit more work to lean into complexity and understand a more complete picture.

Once you commit to understanding the fuller and more complete picture, you may also have to make peace with the new reality that a lot of things no longer have simple answers. This, too, can be challenging. However, acknowledging complexity doesn't mean that you give up or render issues as too hard or unsolvable. In fact, acknowledging complexity means we can do the opposite. If we take each other as complicated individuals, and public issues as being complex and multi-dimensional, we can react with thoughtfulness and a new sense of proportion and perspective, instead of being so quick to rage and hysteria.[78]

The admission that there's more to most things than originally meets the eye also provides you with an opportunity to lower your defences. Once you have loosened your grip on the conclusions you have formed, you no longer need to feel confronted or work so hard to keep conflicting views at a distance. You can instead begin the work of broadening out what you know – looking more widely, considering more fully and inviting more perspectives.

In actively looking for extraordinary educators who are encouraging rethinking by bringing intellectual humility, doubt and curiosity into the way they teach, Grant came across a growing movement in history education of asking questions that don't have a single right answer. The focus, in these discussions, is less about being right, and more about building the skills to kindly consider another's views and argue productively about them.[79] This can result in a windier road to get to a conclusion, but it can take us towards better ones.

My children are learning this at a young age. Better than we did a generation earlier, I would argue. Two of my boys – who are Year 2 and Year 3 at the time I am writing this – engage in this incredible and extra addition to their curriculum called "Philosophy 4 Children" (P4C). Developed by Matthew Lipman in the 1970s, P4C builds on children's natural curiosity and sense of wonder as they explore – through philosophical enquiry – the common, central and contestable concepts that they encounter in their everyday experiences. According to Lipman, 'the students become accustomed to asking each other for reasons and opinions, to listening carefully to each other, to building on each other's ideas'.[80] The skills they learn through P4C – openness to new ideas, developing points of view, expressing ideas coherently, finding relevant examples, respecting others, listening to understand, discussing with objectivity and evaluating context – are then also being applied much more broadly across their other learning. They are developing valuable dispositions around thinking – and they bring home some interesting topics for dinnertime debates.

While we're not necessarily solving all the problems of the world over late-afternoon Lego and lots of lasagne, we are having robust conversations and encouraging them to explore ideas. I can see evidence already of their ability to challenge and probe further. To look beyond the obvious, which is the next aspect required to invite and embrace complexity for the better.

2. Look beyond the obvious

It's one thing to know when you and others are oversimplifying, but the benefit really comes from doing something about it: pushing to dig a little deeper or go a little further, and looking beyond the obvious and the simplistic as we commit to understanding the full picture. The decision-making and problem-solving principle of Occam's razor suggests that we shouldn't use more elements than are necessary to get to an answer, and that when presented with competing hypotheses we should prefer the one that requires the fewest assumptions. To a point this has merit, but somewhere along the way we've come to believe that the simplest explanation is also the most likely to be the truest, or the best one. And we've used this to justify or excuse not looking more closely. It's become a tempting shortcut.

When we fail to account for other contributing factors, however, we're more likely to stay dug in, to perpetuate polarisation, and to run the risk of misunderstanding. To construct an incomplete picture that distorts reality. Real challenges, like real people, are much more complex and complicated than we would like them to be – and it's impossible to arrive at optimal solutions when we start with suboptimal understanding. Bypassing the complexities doesn't mean that they aren't there. We need to broaden out what we know to gain a clear view and to see the full picture, with all its various angles. Anything short of that and we risk missing the mark.

Constructing a clear and comprehensive picture requires us to consciously push past our cognitive biases and thinking tendencies, and to practise disciplined curiosity. We need to dive deeper, look more closely, ask more questions, and uncover further facts. It undoubtedly requires more effort to construct a complete picture, but it's always worth it. Deeper understanding takes us beyond our comfortable fiction and closer towards tackling the often-uncomfortable truths. In order to think better, we need to expand what we know.

When you've identified somewhere that you need to broaden your view, consider the following:

- What research exists already in this field? Is there any angle or aspect missing?
- How strong is the evidence – both for and against – this idea?
- What hasn't been considered yet?
- What if one (or many) of my key assumptions on this are wrong?
- How can I take this idea one step further?
- What are the flow-on effects, or the consequences, of my idea or position?
- Is there anywhere else that this idea is already being applied? What can I learn from that application?

To get us beyond our well-worn thinking ruts, it pays to seek out other perspectives and challenging views, especially from those who think really differently to you. In *The Scout Mindset,* Julia Galef differentiates between a soldier and a scout when it comes to our thinking. Where a soldier's job is to protect and defend, a scout's job is to seek out and understand. These are very different motivations, and they lead to distinct activities. Whereas a soldier's mindset reflects our natural tendency to defend our existing beliefs instead of being open to changing them, the scout mindset brings curiosity, unbiased truth-seeking, and a willingness to face reality – even when that reality is surprising, unexpected, confronting or uncomfortable. It's a willingness to look further, while also taking things as they are.

Make like a scout, and find those who will argue with you. Ask them to poke holes in your argument. Finding real-life humans to engage in respectful verbal sparring is the ideal here, but if you can't engage in real debate, you can engage in the thought experiment. Think about what those who would argue against your idea might say, and explore that with an open mind. Consider how your opposition would frame their position, and commit to finding at least one valid point in what they might raise. Or set out like a scientist and attempt to disprove your own hypothesis.

It can also help to bring a beginner's mindset. While it can be hard to truly imagine what it feels like to not know things that you are already familiar and comfortable with, it's another worthwhile thought experiment for helping you go beyond your current assumptions.

If you put aside everything that you currently know about this problem or issue and approached it fresh, what would you try? Where would you look first? If you were hearing about this for the first time, what would you think? And what would be the questions you would ask first? Again, it's difficult to bring yourself back to being a true beginner, but it's usually possible to talk to somebody else who is one. Start presenting the topic to a true beginner and see how they interpret it and what questions they ask. What approaches might they take? What fascinates them about what you are exploring? And where do they feel like they need more information? Does what you're thinking cover enough bases for them yet? We'll talk more about the beginner's mindset in Chapter 8.

3. Focus your ideas into something workable

The more you increase your understanding of a topic and deepen your expertise, the more complex your thinking becomes. French author and Nobel Prize winner André Gide said: 'One does not discover new lands without consenting to lose sight of the shore for a very long time.'[81] As it is with physical exploring and discovery, so it is with our thinking.

As Pete Davis notes in *Dedicated*,

> When you set out to tell a complex story, your narrative expands outward. You learn about all these new thoughts and ideas, start having all your own thoughts and ideas, and eventually come to know a sprawling cast of characters. In the middle of the process, you panic, because you are stuck in this inchoate mass of ideas – and are already in so deep that you can't get out.[82]

Preparing your ideas to share or proactively deepening your area of expertise can feel like walking into a forest you are excited to explore, but then losing your way as it starts getting denser. Feeling around in the dark is part of the process, but your complicated thinking needs to crystallise into something to enable you to, eventually, find your way.

While leaning into complexity is worthwhile and valuable, we can't stay solely there. It's hard to lead others from such a complicated place. Much like being lost in the forest as night falls, wading around in constant complexity is its own form of torture. If you're an over-thinker like me who has got stuck in thought spirals, you'll know what I mean. So, once you've explored something widely, you need to focus your thinking down, and bring it back to something workable.

I think of the process of leaning into more complex thinking as looking like this.

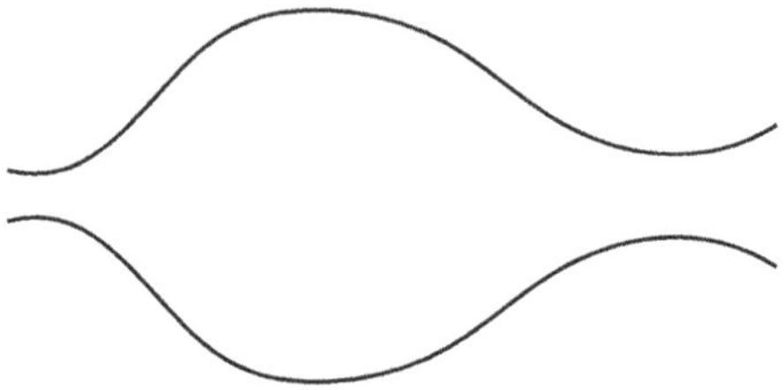

You start on the left-hand side, with the narrow view, and widen that out to include all the possibilities and perspectives you can, before working to focus your thoughts again. You don't want to keep all the complexity in there for the sake of it, or make things needlessly complicated. Some summarising is going to be necessary to make your ideas digestible. You're not aiming for something oversimplified again as you move towards that right-hand side, but you are aiming for something succinct; you want shortened, not basic. You want to refine without reducing, arriving at ideas or working theories that contain the nuance of enhanced understanding, while being something that both you and others can make sense of.

Two tried-and-true techniques will help: talking things through out loud with someone, and writing it all down.

I've already suggested that talking to someone else about your topic can help you to effectively borrow a beginner's mindset, but there's also the simple fact that verbally explaining your ideas to someone forces you to have to organise them. It requires you to structure your thinking as you make judgements about what you share. Even if what you are talking through tends much more closely towards a work-in-progress ramble than a polished and perfected presentation, as you talk it through out loud you get to hear what works, see what gaps you are leaving, and identify the information you need to backfill to help the ideas make sense. You're required to untangle yourself as you're talking, you'll highlight the key points that you want them to understand and remember, and you get to test whether the ideas come across succinctly or where you need to supply more information to supplement others' understanding.

It's also been said that the best way to learn something yourself is to attempt to teach it to others. So, find yourself a confidante or sounding-board. They could be a colleague, a loved one, someone in your industry, or someone completely external from it. The important thing here, however, is to find someone who is willing to listen and attend to your ideas. Knowing that your conversation is finite, and that it can't spiral too far like the thoughts in your head, means you are forced to frame things up, find the most important points, and make choices about what information you share.

Two of the people close to me are fairly direct, sharp-shooters: my colleague, Verity, and my husband, Logan. These two bring me constant reminders of just how differently individuals' brains work. They are both visionary, big thinkers, but they see things much more simply than me. And both are masters at cutting through anything extraneous and quickly paraphrasing back the heart of what I'm figuring out. These two both provide a valuable sounding-board to help me get clear about what I'm thinking. They are like walking, talking summary-machines. And, if I don't like what I hear back, or can see that only a portion of my point is there, I can make some tweaks. They both save me a lot of time spent ruminating, and help me move my thinking forward again when I start spinning my wheels. I would highly recommend finding someone who thinks differently to you, to bounce things around with.

The same sort of prioritising is required when we write things down. On paper (or screen), when we are trying to make a compelling case, we need to organise our thoughts. In *The Extended Mind,* Annie Murphy Paul describes taking notes as something of a cognitive bonus. When we simply watch or listen to information, we may be taking it all in, but we're imposing very few distinctions on the stuff that's coming past our eyes or ears. The same goes for the internal monologues swirling in our minds. When we take notes, she argues, 'we are forced to discriminate, judge and select. This more engaged mental activity leads us to process what we're observing more deeply.'[83] None of us are flawless transcribers, nor are any of us probably fast enough to be, so we make judgement calls on what we will write down as we're listening. As a result, we process the information more as we do this. We also deepen our understanding as there's a high chance that, at least in some of our note-taking, we will paraphrase things into our own words.

Writing can be helpful when we're capturing our own thoughts, too. As Paul attests, note-taking can lead us to having new thoughts. Often it is literally on the page that we do the work – or the thinking as we engage in the cycle of think, draw, look, rethink, redraw.[84] So, pick up a pen and start scrawling.

There's something that gives pen and paper an edge to my mind, and a physicality that helps with focus – but typing up notes is still better than nothing. This still allows you to externalise and examine your thoughts as opposed to just looping on them endlessly in your mind. You can re-read the notes, come back, and build on them, or simply put them aside after you've processed them, if that's all you need. Writing to think is a very different practice than crafting content, too. Don't worry about what the outcome or output of your writing is going to be at this stage, and refrain from editing as you go. Simply trust the process.

Talking things through and writing things down helps us to think more clearly, which is even more important when we've actively followed the road towards the required complexity. When we have broadened out our understanding, we are able to bring things back to size again not by ignoring the complexities, but by actively understanding and appreciating them.

As you review your writing, or reflect on your thinking conversations with others, consider the following:

- What's the most important thing I need to get across?
- If I put my idea into one sentence, what would I say or write?
- If I could choose only one aspect of this to tell someone, what would I share?
- What's the thread that ties all the aspects of this together?

4. Find a fit for the format

When you have the backing of complex and nuanced understanding, you have a more solid and stable foundation from which to lead others with your thinking. Obviously, it's not always practical to write a wordy white paper or a long research report for everything. We can't distil a detailed discussion of every idea we have into a full-length book either; that's unlikely to be practical for you, not to mention those you are here to serve. There are certain formats, and practical reasons, that require brevity. A TED Talk has an upper time limit of 18 minutes – a length chosen by TED organisers based on both neuroscience and strategy. Priding themselves on concise and enlightening talks, the TED team believe 18 minutes to be long enough for a speaker to flesh out an idea, while short enough for the audience to take in, digest and understand all of the important information.[85] Similarly, a LinkedIn post requires 3,000 or fewer characters, however 1,300 to 2,000 characters is the recommended length to maximise engagement and ensure readability.[86] Sometimes, brevity matters.

To be effective, we have to fit the format that will work best for our purposes – whether that be opening up a conversation, encouraging people to think differently, educating people further, or inspiring them to take some action. Not every format is the best way to achieve each end.

In *Think Again,* Grant points to a potential challenge of nuance, which is that it doesn't seem to go viral. It's true that complexity doesn't make for the slickest soundbites, but it does help us to seed great conversations. In the same way that we're trying to get away from black-and-white absolutes or judgements, there is no single rule that works here in all instances. It's not simply the case that longer-form ways of sharing information are inherently more worthy, valuable or virtuous, while shorter formats sell us all short. A balance is preferable. Consider each as having their time and place.

Short-form content captures attention, but it can sacrifice some nuance. Watching a bunch of reels doesn't match the full immersion that you'd get in following the plot of a movie. Reading a series of posts doesn't rival the depth of insight contained in a book. While good thought leadership can't survive on spiffy soundbites alone – and does need to be backed up by substance – it's hard to engage someone to wade through convoluted diatribes and heavy research papers to find the points that you want to make, especially if you haven't done the upfront (and usually more succinct) work to make them want to. Attention spans are short, so we often only have a few seconds to hook someone with a catchy headline, or via those reels or short posts.

Once we have their attention, we can then invite them to engage and explore more deeply. People won't engage with only one type of content either; preferences aren't static. While people might have a favourite format or tend towards one more than others, they will still consume different things on different days, and depending on the mood they are in and what else is going on in their lives.

The best approach is a mix of formats. While you want to be strategic and avoid spreading yourself too thin, don't be defined by one channel or way of getting your thinking out into the world. Constructing the right mix for your ideas is less academic and more intuitive: find what works for you and allows you to be effective. You might look around for examples of others who are succeeding at what you are trying to do and see what works for them. Or test some things yourself, and see what achieves an impact.

Start somewhere, but try not to stay there with too narrow an approach. Add other formats that round out the type of information that you're putting out into the world. You are ideally looking to blend together formats that allow for attention-grabbing and engagement with those that provide more substance and further back up what you're saying. An example could be compellingly crafted social posts that showcase a small amount of your thinking while also posing interesting questions for others. You might also then point to longer-form explorations of your ideas or research reports that are available on your blog or via download from your website. Or it could be that you boil down what you know into a few key lessons contained in a keynote speech (designed to be just 45 to 60 minutes), and then provide much more detail and applied examples of the information via instructional videos, an online or in-person course, or a book that showcases your thinking.

It doesn't matter where you start – longer-form or short and crisp – but you do need to be able to communicate effectively across both long and short formats. This is the sign of great thinking, so see whether your thinking passes this test.

- If you've only got pithy statements and couldn't write a full blog about what you're saying, then chances are there's not enough substance or evidence there yet. Gather stories about your experiences to add weight or consider other perspectives to take your thinking past the territory of simply a "nice saying".

- Conversely, if you can only write long-form and not yet communicate what you're thinking sharply, then you've likely still got some confusion that you need to clear up to put your thinking out in a compelling way. Spend time on some of the suggestions in the previous section for focusing your ideas back down.

Ultimately, we need people to understand our ideas better, so our content, in whatever formats we choose, should avoid confusion. Sometimes this means we have to break things down into smaller bites, and then build up a more complete and complex picture over time. As the previous examples attest, you can absolutely give the high-level insights while providing links or additional documents that contain more information and make more context available. Expose people to your ideas across multiple platforms – recycling what you have to suit each. This is what other seemingly prolific thought leaders are doing.

Ideally you want to strike a balance that enables you to get cut-through while also bringing legitimacy to your leadership and providing substance when people do dig a little deeper or scratch below the surface.

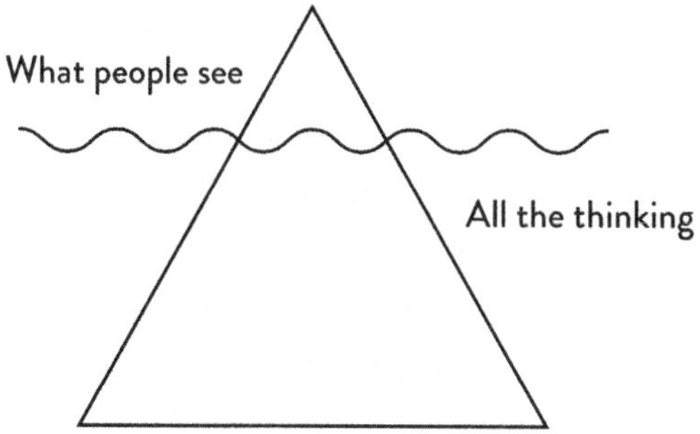

A final note on complexity

While it's hard to create easily digestible content that reflects nuance, one place to start is in considering whether you are indeed embracing complexity, or if you're instead being needlessly complicated.

It's tempting to think that complex and complicated are the same thing, or that complexity is just complication to a higher degree, but there are subtle yet important differences in these terms. Something complicated is cumbersome, overly technical, and hard to figure out or understand. However, understanding it isn't impossible. Tax law is a great example of complication: it's highly technical and difficult to understand, but if you break all the components down, or consult with an expert, full understanding and a solution are possible. On the other hand, something that is complex contains many interdependent elements and/or aspects that are virtually impossible to know for sure – for example, elements that change over time or are unpredictable. Foreign policy is a complex challenge, and while there is no shortage of opinions, there are no clear solutions either.

This is an important distinction. You can present complex arguments without making them needlessly complicated. The key is in how you frame the information that you're putting forward. Embracing complexity often means avoiding absolutes. It means acknowledging uncertainty, as we'll explore in the next chapter. We engage people's interest, while encouraging their curiosity, as we'll also see in Chapter 7. As Myers – the entrepreneur whose thinking we saw near the start of this chapter – urges, we must 'Never mistake simplicity for elegance. All of us, regardless of our calling, must learn to once again embrace deep thinking, complexity, and nuance and reject the temptation to oversimplify. It's time that we embrace a higher calling and push ourselves to thrive in a complex world.'[87]

So far:

When it comes to ideas, it's easy for simplification to go too far. We lose some of the picture and often some of the truth when simple information is put forward not only as fact, but as the full story.

To counter this, we need to invite and embrace complexity where it exists. We need nuance in order to be balanced and better-understanding humans with inclusive and effective solutions. What's more, complex arguments can actually be more compelling and more convincing.

To authentically lean into complexity in service of better:

- identify and resist oversimplification by digging deeper
- look beyond the obvious to get a clearer and more complete picture
- focus your ideas back down, taking them from wide to workable, and
- use varied formats to balance both capturing attention and backing up your claims.

CHAPTER 6

Gaps in our knowledge

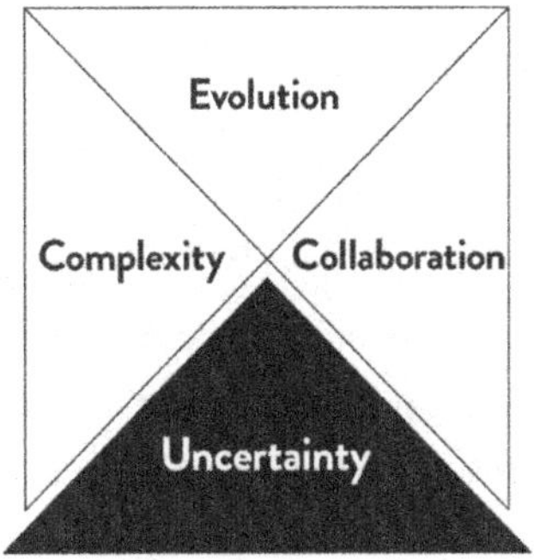

It was hot. It was loud. And the pressure was ratcheting up. It was also just a tad too dark, as a group of friends and I hunched over a bar leaner in the corner of our local pub on Quiz Night, trying to see our answer sheet well enough while also ensuring that others from the surrounding tables couldn't see it.

We were awaiting the MC's next category of questions. We'd been coming here every Tuesday night for a while, now

– my husband and I, with these same friends – to compete for the prized bar tab, to break the monotony of the weekly routine, and to have some fun. We'd definitely achieved the latter, but we'd never come even remotely close to winning the free drinks. All signs pointed to the fact that we should be in with a good shot, especially with my husband, Logan, along – who confidently blurted out answers as soon as each question was asked. He's quick and unwavering, so, assured, we wrote his answers down. Yet, despite our confidence, week after week, we found that we weren't getting an awful lot of answers right. What was going on?

One particular night, I decided to investigate. Responding to a question about the capital city of the Czech Republic, Logan spouts 'Vienna'. I looked around the table. No-one else said anything, and our friend Matt, poised with the pen, started writing. I turned back to Logan.

'Do you actually know that, or are you just guessing?' I asked him, knowing full well that our travels had yet to take us to Europe and that geography is not my husband's strongest suit. He didn't even look sheepish as he confessed that he hadn't really the faintest clue, but it was what popped into his head first, and he had thought it sounded good.

'Okay, that's one possibility …' I said, turning back to the rest of our group. 'Does anyone else know whether that's right or, if not, what the answer could be?' It turns out the answer is Prague; Vienna is the capital of neighbouring Austria.

•••

Speaking with confidence comes naturally to Logan, and he has a direct and compelling communication style, honed through many years as a highly skilled salesperson. Logan doesn't assertively spout off whatever he's thinking in business settings – he actually spends most of his days consulting and asking thought-provoking questions. On these Tuesday nights however, the stakes are low and Logan feels safe in our social circle. (He's also likely to be a pint or so deep by this part of the night.) Add to this context his general self-assuredness and it's-all-under-control demeanour and it's easy for the rest of us to believe what he's saying. Contrast this with how I (who most certainly does not possess this natural style) might venture the same, only marginally certain, opinion about the answer: 'Is it Vienna?' 'Could it be Vienna?' or 'What do we think about Vienna for this one?' Given the answer is incorrect, hopefully we think we should explore further options. And that's the point here.

When we act or speak with confidence, there's less discussion; people will often take what we say to be the truth. However, when we phrase our answer as a question, we invite further consideration and encourage other people to think also. Similarly, when we use hedging language – words like "could", "might", "think" or "guess" – we express ambiguity, caution, indecisiveness, or uncertainty. And this can be a good thing.

Sometimes we simply don't know what we don't know – as is often the case with pub quiz answers. 'What is the name of the oldest lake in the world?' had us well-stumped. (It's Lake Baikal in south-east Siberia.) The same goes in unprecedented times, or when the ground is shifting quickly beneath our feet. It's common, as we embrace greater complexity, that our arguments and our positions become less certain, too. When we attune to the complexities that exist, solutions often become more squiggly, less straightforward. It might not be possible to know all the answers, or at least not yet. And this is okay. We can share what we know and think, while also acknowledging the bits that we aren't sure about yet. Acknowledging uncertainty when we're communicating can be powerful and is another valid way to lead with our thinking.

It makes sense that this idea feels counter-intuitive, or can take a little time to get your head around. We know intuitively, and often from experience, that we appreciate confidence and certainty, but the research also backs this up.

In *Magic Words: What to Say to Get Your Way*, Jonah Berger cites an experiment exploring the choosing of a financial advisor. Participants were told to imagine they had just inherited some money and were looking for an expert to help them invest it wisely. They had already asked friends for recommendations, and found two different advisors equally recommended, so – as the tie-breaker – they were holding a competition. The two advisors had to judge the probability that individual stocks would increase in value over a three-month period. Participants were then able to check both advisor's judgements against the stock's actual performance results and choose which one of them to hire on that basis.

In terms of accuracy, both advisors were equally good – correct and incorrect in their judgements about the same amount of the time. Where they did differ, however, was in how extreme their judgements were. Logic might attest that we'd prefer a more moderate advisor, especially when dealing with the sorts of uncertainty that we encounter in financial markets. However, that's not what the results show. Almost three-quarters of participants preferred the more extreme advisor, despite the fact that they weren't any more "right". People opted for guidance from the person who expressed greater confidence (seen in their more certain predictions), even though this didn't correlate to that advisor's ability to estimate the market trends any more accurately. The researchers concluded that people are more persuaded when those who are communicating seem more certain, or confident about what they are communicating. From this research, Berger surmised that, 'when people speak with certainty, we're more likely to think they are right.'[88]

We're used to leaders speaking powerfully, decisively and with conviction. They seem self-assured, certain and confident, laying things out in a way that makes it hard to imagine any other alternative. As a result, we're more likely to believe them, and not only in a pub quiz setting either.

As I write this, Richard Conway, who we met alongside his inner critic back in Chapter 3, is going through a period of reorganising and reimagining his business amid major industry changes. And while he still believes he needs to set the mood, increase excitement, show his passion, and project confidence to his wider team that they are going the right way, he's also finding more and more occasions where he's better to drop some of that certainty and do a bit more sense-checking. He does this when he consults with other senior leaders in his organisation, actively seeking their perspectives and encouraging collaboration. Because his team are doing the job on a day-to-day basis, he's recognised that they're the best source of practical insights. 'The more knowledge I have, the better decisions I can make,' Richard shares 'and I can only get to those if I'm prepared to ask about the things I don't know yet.'

He similarly has to drop the illusion of having all the answers already with the trusted peers in his entrepreneurial network. In doing so, he's able to bounce ideas off them and receive their advice to build a broader picture. 'I'm vulnerable and candidly honest with this group, leaning on their support and skillsets – and that's hugely valuable,' he shared with me. Richard says that doing this with the market has been another big driver. 'We can't know everything yet, when we're experiencing such significant industry disruption,' he adds. In response, Richard's found the best people in the market globally, employing one of them for a year as a contractor and talking to others – including CEOs of some of the biggest agencies globally – before releasing a six-month pilot scheme with some of his top clients.

As a result of taking other thinking on board, Richard is riding the waves of disruption while maintaining his position at the forefront of the industry in Aotearoa New Zealand. This would not have been possible if Richard had held too tightly onto an "I know it all" façade. 'Even when you are sure of something, new information can sometimes make you pivot or change course. You have to be willing to put aside what you know, or admit you don't know everything with complete certainty,' Richard says.

Academics have similarly proven uncertainty to be worthwhile in the business world when considering strategy. A group of European researchers brought together over a hundred start-up founders for an entrepreneurship training programme.[89] Over four months, these businesspeople learnt to create a strategy for their business, interview potential customers, build a minimum viable product, and refine their prototypes. Despite the training being exactly the same, these businesspeople had been split into two groups: one that did the exercise boldly, as described, and the other that had been told to approach it as a scientist might. The second group were encouraged to see their strategy as a theory, and their customer interviews as a way to further develop or disprove their hypothesis. Creating and testing their product was then viewed as a series of experiments with the aim of revising their hypotheses based on the results.

The start-ups in the "scientific-thinking" group achieved not just double or triple the revenue that the control group averaged; they brought in 40 times the revenue and attracted customers much sooner. Because they viewed their original plans with less certainty, they pivoted more than twice as often as the other group which was much more likely to stay wedded to their original ideas. This wasn't just an academic experiment either. It was based on business results out in the real world. When the study was carried out, the businesses participating were yet to bring in any revenue. This provided an ideal starting point for the researchers to determine the impact that a less-certain mindset might have not just in a research setting, but also on the business's actual bottom line. We expect great entrepreneurs to be clear-sighted and strong-minded, decisive and solid in their convictions. However, the best strategists here were somewhat unsure. They took their time and outwardly demonstrated that they didn't have all of the answers. Because of this, it was easier for them to flex as they needed to change their minds.

Acknowledging uncertainty and opening up discussion is enabling Richard to provide valuable leadership, in turn enabling businesses and entrepreneurs to perform better – and it was enough to improve our pub quiz ranking (though we never did win the bar tab). It's a valid approach, too, in other contexts, especially where we are dealing with ideas and opinions and where we want to move towards better understanding, increased empathy and greater compassion.

You don't need to know everything

The world of leadership is full of numerous half-truths and ever-changing perspectives. One of the common myths that our client Suzi McAlpine sees in her role as a leadership developer is the idea that leaders need to have all the answers. While there are undoubtedly some occasions where a leader needs to quickly and directly assert a course of action, those situations are actually much fewer and farther between than most of us think. More commonly, we could do with a little caution and balance or, at the very least, consultation and collaboration. Suzi urges leaders against falling too quickly into the "compelled to know" camp, and instead suggests that they lean more often into their role as guide for both others and themselves through the territory of not knowing. This approach is particularly valid for thought leaders, especially because the world of ideas is so subjective and experiential, and much is unknown and unknowable.

Suzi recently told me about some work that she'd done with a leadership team to solve a gnarly strategic issue that the organisation was facing. The leadership team had to come up with the direction for the rest of the business, and had, by this stage, spent two hours spinning their wheels. Suzi could see that they were stuck. She was about to jump in, but was proud to instead watch as her client took the initiative and did so. 'Can we just take a pause?' this CEO ventured. 'I sort-of feel like we're going round in circles and we're trying to move into action and problem-solving before we've got alignment on what the problem really is. Is anyone else feeling that, or is it just me?' he went on to say, before adding, 'It's okay if it's just me.' It felt as though everyone in the room let out a collective sigh of relief.

This leader then went on to ask: 'What would be useful for us to focus on now for the next 15 minutes?' He suggested everyone head outside for a couple of minutes of fresh air, and then come back in and answer that. They took the break, before all coming back to the table and determining, with greater collective clarity than they'd had previously, the one question they needed to answer first to move towards a strategic solution.

With a lot of complexity and unknowns that they were navigating, this leader's willingness to admit that he was unsure about their approach was a potent circuit-breaker. Good things happen when we consciously wade deeper into the uncertainty and are prepared to hang out there for a bit. Suzi and I have discussed many examples of leaders approaching their teams with a powerful question and open-minded curiosity around what might emerge, and then, together, coming up with much better answers than what the leader had been circling previously.

Thinking together often leads to thinking better, as we have seen. We have fewer expectations, and are less bound by preconceived ideas. We're also more likely to take risks and explore new avenues. And as we will see shortly, it's often the expression of uncertainty that acts as an invitation to potential collaborators.

However, it's one thing to suggest that those leaders who are already in a position of power ditch the know-it-all persona and ask questions of others; it's another to suggest that those who are trying to build or establish leadership around their ideas put aside what they know straight out of the starting blocks. Surely that's going to undermine any influence that they're able to have? To an extent, certainly: you need some foundation from which to form your position, and we will explore that more shortly. But there is also some scope for not-knowing in there, too, especially when we consider some of the more recent discoveries in the field of influence and persuasion.

Researchers from Carnegie Mellon found an unlikely context where hedging or uncertainty is a more powerful way to communicate: when we are trying to change someone's mind about a controversial issue. In one experiment, David Hagmann and George Loewenstein enlisted hundreds of people to discuss topics where it's common for people to hold vastly different views – issues like whether abortion should be legal, or whether undocumented immigrants who meet certain requirements should be legally permitted to stay in the country, as examples. Contentious topics with complexity, in other words. After sharing their pre-existing attitudes on the issues being discussed, participants read a persuasive message that someone else had written and noted whether it contributed to them changing their minds. Some of the persuasive messages were prefaced by a short note in which the author expressed doubt in their opinion. These notes admitted that, while they had thought carefully about the message they had written and the case they had made, they weren't completely sure that they were right.[90]

Following popular logic, we might assume that expressing doubt in their own view would undermine the persuasiveness that a person might have, and ultimately make them less likely to change anyone's mind. After all, it's hard to be persuaded about something if the person who is meant to be doing the persuading doesn't even seem sure about it themselves. However, the exact opposite occurred. Expressing doubt about a contentious issue increased persuasive power, particularly when the person who was listening had a strongly-held belief. Hearing that someone else wasn't so sure of their position encouraged others to loosen their grip on their own beliefs. They became more likely to change their mind. I'll admit that I had to reread this research a couple of times when I first came upon it; it took me a while to grasp the incredible ramifications this has for how we can argue more productively (and less combatively, which I'm a big fan of!).

While the widely held view is that we're best to be direct and factual when trying to win over someone who currently disagrees with us, it would appear that when we're up against deeply entrenched views we're best not to come at them head-on. Too direct or seemingly sure of ourselves and we can cause the other person to dig in further. You might remember the example earlier of Cain as a young lawyer being thrown in the deep end during a high-stakes negotiation meeting. Her less direct approach felt less forceful than if she had stood up swinging, or pounding on the table – yet it was effective in helping the parties arrive at an outcome that worked for her client. This is good news for those of us who don't feel as though we can communicate in the style or manner that is typified by the dominant archetype.

How do we do it better?

There's solid evidence for why less certain can be more compelling, especially when we consider the fact that persuasion can be broken into two stages. The latter or second stage is where we consider someone else's views or the contrary information that they are presenting to us, and decide whether we will take any of that on board or use it to update our own beliefs. However, before we even get to that point, we must first decide how willing we are to listen. That's the first stage and, unsurprisingly, we're usually wary of people trying to change our minds. It can be destabilising to have our firmly held beliefs challenged, and we often take it as a kind of threat (certainly to our understanding of the "truth"). It's confronting, and uncomfortable.

You've likely experienced this reluctance in your own lives, if you've ever found yourself closed-off to something a presenter or politician was trying to share with you. You may not have done it consciously, but, more likely than not, you made a judgement, early on, about whether you were going to even remain open to what they were saying. Maybe something they said, or something about the way they said it, turned you off from the get-go. Maybe you were bringing other pre-existing information or opinions to the encounter. Perhaps you weren't prepared to challenge the framework (or schema) that you'd categorised them by. Either way, you were simply not having a bar of them. You likely had a logical reason for that. It's not necessarily the case that we are over-confident or holding too tightly onto what we know. We've all got a built-in defence system or anti-persuasion radar that pings us when we can see someone is coming straight at us for the purposes of changing our mind.

It's possible to increase the effectiveness of your position, and increase your persuasive power, by coming at things less forcefully. Let's take a look at how.

1. Embrace the discomfort of not knowing and the fun of learning

When you reframe learning as fun, you take the sting out of what you don't know yet.

First, let's acknowledge that this is a simpler thing to say than it is to do. Because our brains are hardwired to see uncertainty as a threat, it's physiologically normal to feel stress when we come up against things that we don't know.[91] It's also normal to want to avoid this unpleasant feeling. Doing so, however, stops us from learning, growing and, ultimately, performing as well as we could. Leaning into, and being okay with, that uncomfortable feeling of not-knowing, takes conscious work. This is especially the case for ambitious high-achievers who are used to being competent and to understanding things with relative ease.

It is possible to move past this with a couple of minor mindset shifts and some proactive practice. You may have come across this mindset-shifting exercise if you've done work on allaying public speaking nerves. A common piece of advice is to reappraise nervousness as excitement, proving the point that our body doesn't do the work of distinguishing the cause of our over-arousal – instead, our brains make that distinction. The theory goes that if you ascribe a different and more positive meaning to the racing heart, sweaty palms and shallow breathing that occur when you think about getting up on stage – that is, if you view them as signs of your excitement as opposed to the experience of crippling fear – you're more likely to get out there and speak well.

The same can go for how we feel about what we don't know. If we interpret the discomfort of being confronted with new or contrary information as an exciting opportunity to learn or expand our perspective, as opposed to evidence that we've fallen short, then we're going to be better placed to assess and integrate new information and move towards greater understanding and deeper expertise. Shifting from a threat-mindset to an opportunity-mindset is powerful.

It can also help to remember when learning was fun. Think about something that you were once excited to learn – perhaps how to ride a pedal bike without training wheels for the first time, or how to write the name of everyone in your family. My eldest son has been learning to dive into the pool at my parents' house. He's gone from flailing his arms wildly to rocketing in there like an arrow. He's even taken to extending his training further by floating an inflatable ring out in the middle of the pool that he has to dive through, and dragging the spa pool steps over to the edge of the swimming pool to give himself more height to jump from. It's really rewarding to watch, and I can see he's having so much fun trying things out and pushing his limits.

This can also be true for us even in adulthood, since learning something that we are excited about is motivating. When it's to do with your passion or purpose, or an area you care deeply about (as this kid does about the water), then there's engagement, energy, and usually plenty of intrinsic reward up for grabs once you get past the initial discomfort of being a novice. I think it necessarily needs to be this way, too, as learning is rarely a one-off event. More often, it requires dedication and repetition. Trying again and again. Climbing out and diving back in until your teeth are chattering and you're being called out of the pool for dinner. As we'll come to see further in Chapter 8, learning and deepening our expertise is a continual loop.

The thought leaders who I work with who can tolerate uncertainty with the most ease are those who are used to putting themselves in the role of beginner and who actively exhibit curiosity and embrace learning in other areas of their lives, too. One has committed to skiing down the blue-black runs while surrounded by experts, even though she is clearly the slowest one there. She feels the fear, acknowledges that she looks ridiculous, but has decided she's doing it anyway and finds fun and joy in it.

Another has bought a sewing machine and is tackling increasingly complex and demanding projects. Still another has picked up a bass guitar for the first time and taught himself to play it through experimentation, and with the help of some YouTube videos. I have another client who, in his fifties, decided to return to university. And finally, one who throws herself into learning new languages with gusto. She's mastered Portuguese, having picked it up during a stint living abroad in Brazil, and she's achieved proficiency in conversational Italian now, too. If there was ever a good practice in tolerating uncertainty, it's getting to grips with an entirely new-to-you language and culture. (This client also admits that it has taught her that the only way to get really good at something is to be prepared to suck at it first, something I think my skiing friend would also admit!) As we saw in Chapter 4, we don't have to overcome our fear in order to act, we just have to be committed enough to take the leap.

If we think of our openness to learning as a muscle that gets stronger with use, then engaging in learning new things for fun is a powerful way to train. As my lovely language-immersing friend also said, it helps us to develop self-efficacy and build confidence that we can, if not master, then at least make a good go at whatever we put our mind to learning. Strengthening this skill by pushing past the edges of what we comfortably know helps us to practise assessing and integrating the new experiences, evidence and information that we encounter. It's also great practice in paring back our perfectionism, because trying, failing and figuring it out are all necessary steps as we learn. We have to start from somewhere, and it's usually not somewhere good (yet)!

This may seem all well and good in theory when it comes to picking up an instrument or creative project, but for many of us who have built our careers and our identities around what we know, the stakes can feel too high. It's common to struggle with new ideas and thinking when they challenge us in this arena.

My advice is, regardless of the expertise you've already acquired, to approach your topic as though you are still learning. This can then help you to feel less threatened or destabilised when you encounter contrary beliefs or conflicting evidence and opinions out in the world. It enables you to swap out the discomfort of not knowing everything for the fun that this opportunity presents.

2. Establish your solid ground – the scope of what you do know

While embracing learning as fun can help, we will ultimately feel safer to lean into the discomfort of uncertainty when we can securely back what we do know. To find confidence in what you know, you need to draw from your experience and evidence base to ensure you have a solid foundation, while also acknowledging what you don't know (yet). This can help you to lower the stakes considerably. And you're going to do that by approaching your knowledge and expertise more like scientists do.

Science is an inherently forward-thinking field: it's effectively a process of encountering uncertainty while exploring the unknown, increasing our understanding of the world, and answering new questions. However, scientists don't just stumble around lost in the dark, and bump into whatever is in their way. Nor do they curl up into the foetal position and rock quietly in the corner because they are crippled by doubt. Instead, they have a plan for what they are trying to prove and disprove, and a systematic approach to isolating the known knowns (the things that are understood well) and the known unknowns (the things we are aware we don't yet understand).

In Chapter 3, we looked at the experience we've gained, and how we've been testing the hypothesis that we can make something better. The known knowns are the things we can take for certain. This forms the basis of your solid foundation. But they're not all you have to contend with. There are also the known unknowns – the things you are aware of but don't (yet) understand. For example, Richard can be certain that his services are helping businesses to grow online, but he doesn't (and can't) yet know all the ways that artificial intelligence (AI) will change that or his clients' businesses.

When your understanding about something is relatively rudimentary or surface-level, everything seems relatively simple. As your expertise deepens, and as you branch into additional aspects or invite more complexity, you wade into greater uncertainty. 'The more you know, the more you realise you don't know,' attributed to Aristotle, points to the fact that as you learn more about something, you come to see the vastness of possible knowledge there is to uncover about that thing – a magnitude that seems impossible to master. There's a tendency to encounter many more known unknowns as you get to know more about a topic area, and you become aware of other variables and interdependencies that you may not fully understand yet.

In *Raising Critical Thinkers,* author and educator Julie Bogart explains this further, asserting that 'the more we engage with a topic for study, the more nuance and intimacy we discover'.[92] This is where scientists look to for opportunity; they are skilful in navigating this phenomenon that I refer to as the "reverse expertise trap". However, I've seen increasing uncertainty all-too-often derail aspiring thought leaders – and I've had it derail me (plenty of times, if I'm honest!). As we engage more deeply with a topic, and add experience to our understanding, we're met with things that reassure us that we're on the right track – promising results, agreement or further evidence of what we're thinking from others – but there are often also unexpected insights that challenge us.

While I was writing this book, I talked to so many people who nodded and smiled when I talked about reluctance, and I heard so many stories of how that was showing up for them. However, I also talked to people who – while agreeing with a lot of what I was talking about – were still steadfast in their belief that they had to be careful not to show too much uncertainty, fearing that people wouldn't follow them if they perceived them to be unsure. One person pointed to the limiting effects of Aotearoa New Zealand's pervasive "tall poppy syndrome" that sees us conflate confidence with arrogance and encourages us to be self-effacing. He believed we couldn't go into a market like the United States with our Kiwi humility, claiming that it's not quaint and appealing, and that we're undermining ourselves if we don't adopt a bigger and more bolshie persona.

As was the case for me in these conversations, our inner critics get louder when we start doubting ourselves. Many turn to the acquisition of more knowledge in an attempt to ward this off. This approach is not a bad thing. Scientists do it, too, by designing more experiments, doubling-down on their research, and opening up new avenues of study. The uncertainty fuels them. However, I can't tell you how many research rabbit holes I followed and then got stuck down on the road to writing this book. And similarly, for many other thought leaders in the making, the doubts that come from bumping up against something they don't know or don't agree with stoke their reluctance to put their thinking out there. It's natural to reason that, just one more article, just another hour of research, another conversation, or another qualification will mean an aspiring thought leader will figure it all out and stop feeling like an imposter. But sometimes you've got to bite the bullet and back what you do know, as one of my fellow authors in our Better Book Project told me. If you start from solid ground you need not defer putting your thinking out there, and you no longer need to trap all the valuable knowledge that could be helping others in your head.

To get your stable ground, find the edges of what you know and understand, and then appreciate the things that still sit outside of that. You can create a sort of "ignorance-base" – some form of a database or list of all the things you don't know or fully understand just yet, which then provides direction for your next discoveries. This way of cataloguing it all is freeing and presents an opportunity. Armed with your list, you can relax about feeling like you need to have all the answers before you can lead with your thinking. You move many unknown unknowns into being known unknowns, when you're conscious of the edges of your current knowledge. And with that, you are able to start. You've got a map of where you need to go next and can trust that you will figure out more of the finer points as you go.

The other positive for acknowledging the outer edges of what we know is that it helps us to bring humility to our work. When we're novices, we're less aware of our limitations – more prone to over-confidence, as we saw back in Chapter 3. Expertise and self-awareness help us to develop right-sized humility.

In *Think Again,* Adam Grant clears up a common misconception about humility. Distinct from being a matter of low self-confidence, or something that keeps us stuck (which it can do if it's over-played), humility actually means, at its root, being grounded. It recognises that we are flawed and fallible. In its most helpful guise, it's an open acceptance of our limitations and a commitment to evolving. I see it, too, as an acknowledgment that we're still learning – staying both curious and humble in our pursuit of more knowledge.

Grant distinguishes between confidence as a measure of how much you believe in yourself, and how much you believe in your methods. As he puts it: 'You can be confident in your ability to achieve a goal in the future while maintaining the humility to question whether you have the right tools in the present.'[93] I would also add that it's not just tools in the physical sense; you can question whether you yet have all the knowledge or information required also. And in fact, you should.

When we have our solid ground of base-level competence, then awareness of our limitations is helpful in avoiding the blindness (and other negative elements) of the over-confidence trap that we looked at in Chapter 3. As Tomas Chamorro-Premuzic says in *Why Do So Many Incompetent Men Become Leaders?*: 'When competent individuals lack confidence, they will prepare more, act with caution, and become more aware of potential risks and obstacles, all of which enhance their performance. When confident people lack competence, their best bet is to hide it from others.'[94]

Think about how this might play out at work, when you're called to contribute your opinion about a new policy or the validity of a business case. You've got some initial thoughts, but aren't 100 percent certain yet on a recommendation. So, you take a little bit more time. You review the details of the business case more attentively. Perhaps you talk to some of your colleagues who will most be impacted by the eventual outcome of what's being considered. Either way, you prepare more extensively, and really think things through – considering and assimilating feedback and, overall, more thinking inputs – before venturing your opinion. What you do eventually put forward demonstrates higher-quality thinking and more robust reasoning as a result. Equally, you might see this in action with others in your team. That colleague who is slow to speak up in the meeting, but who always has something insightful to say when they do venture to contribute. They've spent more time listening and processing; their opinion is considered and perceptive.

Slower and less certain can lead us all to better outcomes. Of course, we need to find a balance between action and reflection, since there's little value in finally getting your opinion out after a decision has already been made and your colleagues have all moved on. What we're aiming for is confident humility – some measure of belief in our capability and our ability to learn or move towards mastery, with enough doubt to encourage us to examine old knowledge and motivate us to acquire more where we are lacking.

In *The Art of Insubordination,* Todd Kashdan talks about how deliberate humility makes us wiser, since 'wisdom arises from understanding the limitations of our own knowledge, respecting others' viewpoints, remaining open and receptive to criticism, and communicating our ideas respectfully'.[95] This echoes my deepest hope for a better and broader version of thought leadership: seeing more people standing up with what they do know, being okay with and upfront about what they don't know, and staying committed to what they are still working to figure out – all while using their unique combination of gifts to bring value to the world. We need great thinkers who have valuable things to say to both back what they know, and be open about what they don't in a way that adds to, as opposed to underminies, their position.

When you're brave enough to venture what you do know out there, magic happens, and your thinking gets better. Engaging more deeply around something, and adding further experience and perspectives to your understanding, develops your ideas further. When you put your thinking out there, you are testing out what you know, which can be destabilising, but is always productive. You find evidence that could lead you down a different path, or discover aspects that you hadn't considered yet, and all of that improves where you're going.

3. Approach new knowledge like a scientist might

I said before that scientists can navigate the reverse expertise trap artfully. They do this, according to one scientist – Dr Stuart Firestein, neuroscientist and chairman of the Department of Biological Sciences at Columbia University – because they view ignorance, as opposed to knowledge, as the true engine of science. Scientific discovery, as he describes it, is more akin to 'feeling around in dark rooms, bumping into unidentifiable things, looking for barely perceptible phantoms'.[96] Worried that his students would feel they understood the brain once they had read the 1,400-plus-page textbook, Firestein set out to make it very clear that science does not have all the answers. Instead, as he argues in *Ignorance: How It Drives Science*, many scientific facts aren't solid or immutable, but are instead destined to be vigorously challenged and revised by successive generations.[97] And although this might seem like a confronting notion for some of us, it's an exciting driver for scientists who feel less internalised pressure to have all the answers because they are used to confronting unknowns as an essential part of the scientific process. Scientists are, ideally, curious, humble and willing to test a hypothesis, rather than assume it's right.[98]

When scientists design an experiment, they set the scope of what they are studying: they outline what they think now, as well as what they don't yet know, and what they hope to discover. They look for connections to other research, use small questions to get at big ones, and tackle some problems simply out of curiosity. Perhaps most importantly, they approach what they are doing as an experiment with the purpose of learning. This is what we need more of. Solutions to complex challenges are only likely to emerge through trial and error, and that requires the willingness to act, the humility to learn, and the ability to adapt.

But none of this applies only in the scientific world. It's true for new discoveries, but it's also true for creativity. Ed Catmull, founder of Pixar, said: 'There is a sweet spot between the known and the unknown where originality happens; the key is to be able to linger there without panicking.'[99] We can take this mindset and approach to any complex issue. We are always learning and, as such, we should be always revising our understanding and our theories. Despite the fact that scientific principles and work have expanded our knowledge so dramatically in the past couple of centuries, there are still many mysteries. Firestein and his supporters believe that teaching people only about the scientific discoveries that are proven is not enough.[100] He now teaches a class on scientific ignorance, and invites scientists from diverse fields to come and lecture. He asks them specifically not to share about their discoveries. Instead, he wants them to come and share what they don't know.

We need to showcase areas of certainty and those where inquiry is still ongoing. In the scientific world, those defending a theory who are faced with an anomaly must revise and modify their theory to eliminate any conflict. If there are enough anomalies, the old theory is replaced with a new, better one.

Kashdan has a valuable reminder here, too: he urges readers to train themselves to behave more like scientists when encountering different yet worthy ideas, as opposed to lawyers who seek to bury any information that conflicts with pre-existing conclusions. 'Remember you're *supposed* to update your belief system as you encounter new information. That's how you grow!' he adds.[101]

We lose out when we profess to know more than we do and believe our knowledge to be solid and stable because it's the *not* knowing, the puzzling over thorny questions, that propels us forward. As Firestein says: 'People tend to think of not knowing as something to be wiped out or overcome, as if ignorance were simply the absence of knowledge. But answers don't merely resolve questions; they provoke new ones …' Often it's in exploring the things we don't know that new discoveries – and magic – happens.[102]

4. Disarm defensiveness and be upfront about the holes in your argument

Finally, it's not just about thinking like scientists in embracing uncertainty, it's about reporting like them, too. You don't need to profess to know everything, and, in fact, it's better if you don't – not only so that you can move your knowledge further, but also so that you can inspire better thinking, or rethinking, in others also. It's okay to be upfront about the things you're still working on and working out, and where you're straying into, or bumping up against territory that you don't yet know so well. When you're working to expand or change the thinking of others, which is in large part the role of a thought leader, then expressing doubt helps.

As we saw earlier in this chapter, admitting the ways in which we're uncertain, or perhaps conflicted, can help to lower others' defences. And the research taking place in the Difficult Conversation Lab that we saw in Chapter 5 provides proof that, in communicating your thinking, you'd do well to acknowledge the many factors or perspectives at play – something that can also be a way to define the limits of your knowledge. One reason that this approach works is due to the surprise factor. We don't necessarily expect knowledgeable people to admit doubt, so, when they do, we tune in and pay more attention to the substance of their argument. It encourages us to look at how certain we are about what we're thinking, too. It makes them seem less threatening (as well as less arrogant). And, powerfully, expressing doubt about our own view shows a willingness to embrace how complex something is, an openness to other perspectives, and an acceptance that conflicting beliefs might be valid – all of which positively models and invites others to do the same.

Even if we don't consciously know it, we tend to match ourselves, in large part, to the people we are interacting with. Research has shown that we physically mirror other people's body language during social interactions.[103] It's called "limbic synchrony", and it signals connection during conversation. But have you noticed the tendency and temptation we have to also match someone's tone (especially someone we want to be on the good side of)? You've likely experienced or even used this strategy in your own interactions. It's hard to remain level-headed about a topic when someone enters a discussion with all guns blazing: our heckles come up almost immediately.

Similarly, you can diffuse high emotions if you refuse to rise up to meet them, and instead remain calm and even. The fire quickly goes out of someone spoiling for a fight if you refuse to fight back. These examples might seem extreme (and perhaps more combative than necessary), but they make the point. You can't ultimately control how open or receptive someone will be to what you are saying, but when people know that something is uncertain, pretending it's not can backfire. It undermines our ability to persuade. In some situations, the best course of action can be to express doubt.

In validating how tricky the thinking is around a particular issue, or how much there still is to discover, you approach the topic and other people with your defences down and you encourage them to lower theirs also.

When we see a scientific study, or a peer-reviewed piece of academic work, it's commonplace to also see the limitations of the work. It's very explicitly stated what the scope of a particular piece of research was, and what we can infer from the results of the study and what we cannot. The authors outline any assumptions that were made. However, we rarely find these sorts of frames or disclaimers around our less formal discourse. It's time that we should. We need experts who will go deep, but we can't all go deeply down every rabbit hole – there are always barriers and limitations. Everybody needs a frame. So share where your case might still be falling short, or where there could be holes in your argument. Not in an apologetic way, but with humility (and a bit of humanity).

We need more inquiring, adaptive and on-its-way-to-great thinking out there. Just as scientists and academics are upfront about what you can fairly conclude, and what you can't safely derive from the results of their studies, you can point to places where you can back up your assertions (and the evidence you've gathered) and acknowledge where you're on shakier ground.

One of our clients and authors, Stanley Henry, is currently doing this as he develops the content for his first book. While Stan has, or has had, hundreds of high-profile clients who provide the evidence that first growing an audience – or in Stan's lingo, 'attracting attention' – is a valid business model, Stan knew he was on shakier ground when it came to a foolproof formula for how that then translates into value and revenue. His clients and readers don't just want followers for the sake of followers (in other words, attention in order to just be making noise), they want to be able to monetise them – turning their large followings into a business.

Stan has made the leap from followers to income himself, and has seen vast attention become income for countless clients. But when I pressed him further on the why and how, he knew he needed more. 'I can trust it, but I can't explain it,' Stan admitted in our first workshop together. So, as well as diving deeper into behavioural psychology research, he's going out to his almost 1 million followers and admitting what he doesn't know in case they can help him explain it. In using himself as the ultimate case study, he's mining his own followers for insights into how others can also create a tribe of followers with high enough trust that they could sell them anything. He's building a more robust case and winning over the sceptics – me included.

Pointing to uncertainty helps us in taking care not to go beyond what we know for sure, and, when we use it as a means of seeking input, then it helps us to extend our knowledge base. As Grant points out: 'An informed audience is going to spot the holes in our case anyway. We might as well get credit for having the humility to look for them, the foresight to spot them, and the integrity to acknowledge them.'[104] Doing this, while admitting and committing to the fact that you are continuing to explore further, can inspire greater trust.

This is something Grant addresses in his earlier book, *Originals*, where he outlines entrepreneur Rufus Griscom's approach to front-footing the weaknesses in his business when presenting to investors, which in turn made him more credible when he then talked about the business's strengths. Griscom included, upfront, a slide that outlined the five reasons not to invest in the company, and says this about his approach: 'You need confidence to be humble, to front-run your weaknesses. If I'm willing to tell them what's wrong with my business, investors think "There must be an awful lot that's right with it".'[105]

Showing the holes or edges of your argument can improve others' perceptions of what you are asserting – and, as we'll see in the next chapter, it can invite participation, too. All of this is, I hope, freeing. When you understand this, you can relax on feeling that you need to know *all* of the answers before you can start putting your valuable thinking out there. Instead, you have permission to start. And just as Stan is demonstrating, you can figure out some of the finer points as you go, all while adding value to the people you are here for.

So far:

You do not need to know everything. While communicating confidently and decisively makes it seem like we know what we're talking about, it's possible to increase our persuasive power and still carve out a firm position while coming at things less forcefully.

Acknowledging uncertainty when we're communicating can be equally powerful and can lead to better outcomes.

To authentically lean into uncertainty in the service of better, follow these steps:

- Reframe learning as fun so that what you don't know yet becomes an opportunity as opposed to a source of discomfort.
- Find confidence in the solid ground of what you do know. And then approach things you are less certain of with humility.
- Expand on your natural curiosity by approaching new knowledge like a scientist does. Discovery is where the magic – and the progress – often happens.
- Disarm defensiveness in others by proactively outlining the edges or scope of your knowledge.

CHAPTER 7

Consultative as a style

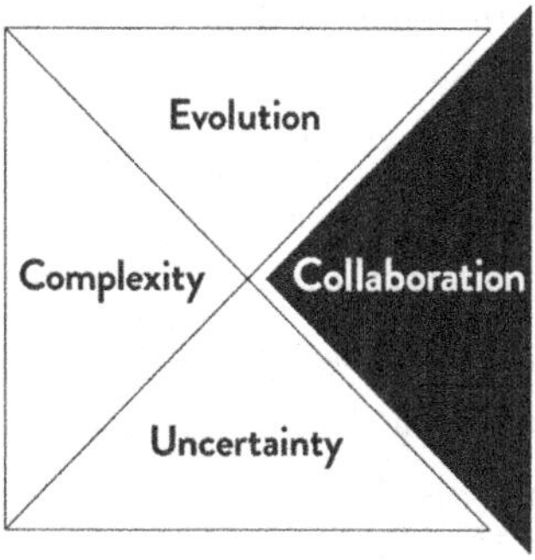

I was in a café on Auckland's North Shore having an afternoon cup of tea with one of my very clever and successful yet incredibly humble clients, Richard Conway – who you've already heard about in Chapters 3 and 6. Richard was one of the original people who made me think of the reluctant thought leader label. Uncomfortable with self-promotion, Richard would have much preferred to be a peripheral character. However, Richard has – ever since his start-up days – believed that raising his profile was one of the best and most budget-friendly ways to build a business. He's pushed himself out there and proven this thinking right.

This particular meeting was a welcome reprieve, I believe, as Richard was otherwise deep in preparing a keynote speech that he'd been invited to deliver about a topic that he was still establishing his knowledge in. It was adjacent to his primary area of expertise, and still very much an emerging field (in other words, it contained a lot of unknowns, and many unknowables). Locking eyes with me across the top of his teacup, Richard admitted that he was worried whether he knew enough to speak definitively about the topic. I challenged him on whether he needed to.

Even though he was going to be the one up on stage holding the microphone, he didn't need to stand up as the expert in every aspect of this complex topic. Or rather, he didn't need to stand up and profess to have all the answers. Instead, he could bring what he did know a lot about and encourage others' curiosity by showing what there still was to discover, I suggested. He could pose some thought-provoking questions, explore multiple sides of the issue, and encourage the audience to think about what they could apply to their own lives and work. 'That's still leadership,' I insisted.

We talked about the huge value there could be in doing that, although he admitted that it felt like a brave move. After all, he'd been given the speaking slot because he's meant to know things, right? And he does. He knows a lot of things; his expertise in his subject area, and his work starting to explore this topic, are what had gained him the opportunity. But there would be another huge benefit if he took the approach I was suggesting: he'd leave a lot of room for others if he presented as though he didn't know all the answers.

The day of the presentation rolled around and Richard's speech went off without a hitch. He leaned into story-telling, and talked about his own journey and how he and his team had experienced this new technology so far. He shared his predictions – labelled as "best guesses" – of where he thinks it's going to go next. And his talk landed fabulously. Not only did he receive lots of positive feedback, but there's been more engagement with Richard's ideas since, and he's been able to start, and continue, other related discussions following the event.

•••

When we present our thoughts and ideas with less certainty, and when we show the complexities that perhaps we haven't solved yet, we leave room for others. The role of a leader is to encourage and inspire others; a leader is there to act as a guide and coordinate the efforts of those in their team towards a desired outcome. So, if you're a leader in thinking, your job is to lead with your thinking – but it's also to lead others' thinking, too. That's what it's going to take to have an impact and create change. The goal is not to be crowned a "guru", so you don't actually need to have all the answers readily to hand. As a thought leader, you are also there to provoke thought. In a world where so many claim to know it all already, and where they're holding their opinions tightly, and often with dire consequences, we need more humble thought leaders who will say, 'Hey, we're still figuring this out – but let's do it together.'

We're better off when we put our minds together to think or problem-solve. I see this daily within my team, as well as in the course of our work with clients. In providing a sounding board, we are encouraging others to defend, better explain, and, in the process, deepen and evolve their ideas. And in the course of our work, we lend others our perspectives, we challenge thinking biases, and we see things that our clients – absolutely experts in their own rights – might have assumed, or simply missed because of the depth of their expertise.

I also see evidence of the power of sharing our thinking to improve and evolve ideas when we get out from behind-the-scenes and engage in helping others do the work to build thought leadership. They venture ideas that get challenged, added to, or applied differently to how they might have intended – all of which leads them to continually improve and mature what they're thinking. In this way, good thought leadership is a conversation. As we will see in the next chapter, it's an ongoing work-in-progress also. There's a virtuous cycle that's created when we approach thought leadership this way, when we're deep in doing the thing that we're leading the thinking around, and when we engage others in the development of our ideas.

Some of the reasons why can be found in Carl Weiman's research. A Nobel Prize-winning physicist and professor, Wieman was grappling with the challenge of getting undergraduates in his classes to understand physics the way he could understand physics, so that they could then begin to truly think like physicists. It didn't seem to matter how he communicated or demonstrated the concepts, his students' ability to solve physics problems remained basic and rudimentary.

He ultimately found the answer for how to turn a hesitant or halting thinker into a skilful or dexterous one – not in his undergraduate students, but in the graduate students who came to work in the lab. When his PhD candidates started, they were much like his other students: their thinking was similarly narrow and rigid. However, look forward a year or two and they had evolved into the types of flexible thinkers that Weiman was trying to create many more of. He looked at what happened in the research lab that was missing from the classroom before concluding that a major factor in his graduate students' transformation was 'their experience of intense social engagement around a body of knowledge – the hours they spent advising, debating with, and recounting anecdotes to one another'. Social interaction appeared to be an essential facilitator of intelligent thought, and Weiman went on to set up his subsequent college classes in a way that facilitated a very different, debate-based intellectual process.[106]

Thought leadership should be a conversation

If social interaction is an essential facilitator of intelligent thought, this means that it's a problem if we keep our thinking hidden until we feel like it's all figured out and finished. Yet so many of us think and act this way. What Weiman discovered, and has spent the subsequent years of his career working to advance, was that 'the development of intelligent thinking is fundamentally a social process'.[107] Of course we can, and do, engage in thinking on our own, but our brains have evolved to think with people – to teach them, to argue with them, to exchange stories with them. Just like Weiman's student researchers were doing. Ultimately, it was his finding that when we think socially, we think differently, and often better.

It isn't just Weiman who has figured this out either. Cognitive scientists Hugo Mercier and Dan Sperber further support this idea, pointing out that we did not evolve to solve tricky logic puzzles on our own.[108] What we did evolve to do, they assert, is persuade other people of our views, and use reasoning to evaluate the justifications and arguments of others. Reasoning is a social activity that works best in context with others, and not so well in solitary use. In fact, it's rare that we are able to arrive at better beliefs and decisions on our own, compared to when we think with others. We are natural-born arguers, Mercier explains.[109] A range of studies show that when people fight over ideas, and do so with mutual respect, they are more productive and creative. Remember, we're aiming for active, informed and respectful debate. We cannot solve problems with the same mind, or the same level of thinking, that created them. Engaging others enables our thinking to evolve.

Many of us know that we arrive at better, more inclusive outcomes when we involve others in our thinking. That's why many of our thinking practices involve other people. We brainstorm in groups to generate more creative ideas. We share what we're thinking for our influence to grow and spread. When we put our ideas out there, they have room to expand, be picked up by others, and grow into something much bigger than we might have previously imagined. We ask those who we trust for advice or for another perspective when we're feeling stuck, and we consult with people we're designing solutions for, to increase our chances of hitting the mark.

In fact, there's a whole field based around customer-centric design that has emerged to ensure we're not working toward creating things that reflect only the way that *we* think they should be, but that we're also considering other users' needs. The same goes when we are thinking about ideas. Being creative together can result in tremendous, transformative collaboration that far exceeds our expectations and our solo efforts.[110] Our thinking is better when we consider that there is more than one point of view, and when we truly understand the problems and realities of the people who we want our ideas to benefit.

Collaboration is a powerful encourager of empathy. When you enlist others, you increase your ability to understand their feelings, thoughts and perspectives. You bring in more views and influences, as opposed to relying on yours alone. When we do this with our ideas, we enhance our understanding of where others are starting from when they encounter our thinking.

Empathy is also the first step towards inclusion and enrolment. If we want to arrive at solutions that work for and benefit the biggest possible group of people, then the thinking that gets us there needs to be empathetic and inclusive. We must set aside our own opinions and assumptions while we seek the perspectives and input of others. If you've ever worked in a large corporate where core values, set by a small and select group of senior managers, are handed down through the organisation, then you will have some idea of how this goes. Defining the values is one thing; deeply ingraining them into the organisation's culture so that they will drive the desired behaviours and business outcomes is quite another. Contrast this with the process of a group or team consulting together and co-creating the operating procedures and values that they want to drive their behaviour, and the result is as different as night and day in terms of agreement and adoption. Research into consultative management styles has also found that, while consultation can be more time-consuming and can slow down decision-making, it improves the quality of decisions, since more inputs are considered and greater creativity around solutions is stimulated.[111]

We love to be asked for our input and it's in our nature to want to improve things. In *The Song of Significance,* Seth Godin points to studies that show that when we ask people 'How can this be different?', more than 90 percent of respondents will suggest something to make the idea better. And this was the case across the globe. It seems we're simply wired to make things better.

There's a beautiful example of this from outside of the business world also. In the Baha'i faith, people who do not crave attention and power are valued; the faith actively works to constrain the ego and induce unity. In their meetings, they follow a protocol of consultation, which is designed to allow people to speak their mind without getting too attached to their own brilliance. Once an idea is shared, it becomes the property of the group (it's no longer just about the original thinker anymore) and, as a result individuals feel less need to defend their ideas if others offer up alternatives or criticisms.[112] There's a lot that we can learn and draw parallels from here.

In a similar way, thought leaders learn to relax their grip on their ideas. In genuinely and generously sharing what they know, they start or progress the conversations that we have around ideas. They bring new perspectives or information into the conversations that are taking place, and, in this way, they humbly move what we know and are able to do forward.

A conversation is a two-way street, of course, requiring us to exchange information and ideas. However, we often default back to the poised figurehead as leader, who knows and imparts all of the wisdom and instructions. We've already seen the arguments for acknowledging how much there is to know, and admitting that we can't possibly have total understanding of it all. However, too many still fall prey – as my client Richard did around his keynote – to the pervasive, all-knowing leader archetype. Embodying this seems to be the default setting; it's extremely rare to see political leaders express uncertainty and seek others' input, especially publicly. Like the sage on the stage, they pass their ideas off as facts.

This is what the dominant model of thought leadership has conditioned us towards. In *Think Again,* Adam Grant shares research that reveals that when a speaker delivers an inspiring message the audience scrutinises the material less carefully and forgets more of the content. Social scientists call this the "awestruck effect", and it's a common phenomenon when we are faced with charisma and certainty from clever presenters who profess to know it all. This is especially a problem if it's the majority, or total, of what we're exposed to. We should be persuaded much more by the substance of an argument, as opposed to the shiny package it's delivered in. We should be judging the merit of ideas by how much value they provide. However, that's harder to do when we're awestruck. Grant labels the phenomenon instead as "the dumbstruck effect". To his mind, 'the sage-on-the-stage often preaches new thoughts but rarely teaches us to think for ourselves'.[113] And as we've now seen, that isn't really, at its heart, thought leadership.

We want thought leaders who encourage us to engage with better and different thinking, who promote openness and generosity, and who distribute power to many. They can take a position, of course – but a big part of the role of a thought leader is to help us apply their ideas to our work or our lives.

Looking again to leadership

While I still absolutely believe that the most effective leadership approach depends on the specific situation, as we explored in Chapter 4, I am encouraged that more consultative styles are now being better valued and utilised alongside the traditional, top-down styles. The "command and control" approach wins the day in a crisis, however critics of this approach claim that it favours compliance over creativity, and stifles experimentation and innovation (which we know is what ultimately moves us forward towards better outcomes).[114] In the context of thought leadership, too, this authoritative style does not create the environment for the best thinking and solutions. Nor is it encouraging engagement, which is what we need if we hope to open the door to change.

When people are treated as passive followers rather than active participants, their motivation and commitment diminish. What we need instead, and what we've seen a shift towards in leadership more generally, is more democratic or consultative styles that improve communication and buy-in, and lead to better decision-making and greater success for organisations.[115] Engagement comes when people are encouraged to participate in processes, asked to share their opinions, and shown that their input is valued and heard. We're more bought into something when we have participated in its creation or development. That's one of the reasons for the huge up-tick in crowdsourcing – the process of inviting ideas from groups – by organisations. They're using it as a way to increase employee engagement and collaboration across department lines, and it's empowering people with a new means to affect change within their organisations.[116]

Consultative leadership – also referred to as participative leadership – values independent thought and assumes that team members have capability and knowledge. This is a useful starting point when we want to engage others with our ideas. When you lean into a more consultative approach, you're assuming and trusting that your audience or followers have capability and knowledge, too.

We can see this mirrored in an educational environment where the sage on the stage terminology originally emerged. This strategy is only one part of the story, and the subsequent shift in education has similarly been towards a more consultative and collaborative approach, referred to as the "guide on the side" approach. While the sage might command attention, the guide gives students or listeners more agency. In a traditional lecture, the teacher (or expert) is the one talking, and the students take notes or passively absorb the material, committing as much as they can to memory so that they are ready to regurgitate it on request. With the guide approach, people are encouraged to think rather than memorise, based on the theory that this encourages students to take deeper ownership of the learning process and make a more meaningful connection with the material.[117]

The "guide on the side" method requires greater engagement

and participation, which counters some of the challenges around both memory retention and critical thinking ability that are rife when we're awestruck or dumbstruck. Learning based on active engagement and critical thinking promotes understanding and excitement.[118] As Grant points out: 'By asking questions rather than thinking for someone, we invite them to join us as a partner and think for themselves.'[119]

In Chapter 5, we saw how Google's model may be affecting our ability to think, and there's another example of the impact of technological innovations here. In his book *The Shallows: What the Internet is Doing to Our Brains*, Nicholas Carr writes that 'the more that people depended on explicit guidance from software programs, the less engaged they were in the task and the less they ended up learning.'[120] The logic goes that the more we "outsource" thinking and problem-solving to others – be they machines or other people – the more we reduce our brain's abilities to learn and later apply ideas.

Greater consultation helps to embed our insights better, and gives them greater applicability, which is what we need for impact. It also helps us to dismantle the all-knowing archetype, which is a good thing for helping reluctant thought leaders to get started.

How do we do this better?

A consultative style really shines in inspiring participation. This dovetails with what we explored in the previous chapter around uncertainty. When we don't profess to know all the answers, we leave room for others. People don't typically feel inclined to engage in constructive dialogue if the other party isn't going to do so, or if they profess to already have all the answers. Collaborative or consultative communication is less threatening, and more inviting. It's also more generous. When we're focused on serving people, far more than defending our territory, it's easier to listen to others. Adopting this mindset, and taking a collaborative approach, enables you to show that you are open – welcoming of input and challenge, and prepared to listen and suspend your initial judgements.

When thought leadership is a conversation, it creates space for others to pitch in. In order to authentically lean into a consultative style in service of better, you will increase your comfort in collaboration and incomplete knowledge, and consciously create a community of people whose input you value and whose ideas and perspectives you can draw from.

1. Enlist others, and ask for advice

It's commonly acknowledged that leadership can be lonely. It's especially isolating when you believe that you need to solve all the problems and come up with the right answers all by yourself. Many business owners I spoke to had that experience amid the near-constant change and challenging uncertainty of the Covid pandemic. Similarly, I have found that, when the complexity and volume of my workload increases, and I veer dangerously close to overwhelm, my natural tendency is to double-down my focus and individual efforts. While this inward retreat may feel like a useful strategy in the short-term, it tends to be a disaster when it's our only response. Instead, as Rebecca Zucker and Darin Rowell writing for *Harvard Business Review* attest, it's in times of change, challenge, uncertainty and overwhelm that it's most important that we reach out to our networks and beyond for insight and perspective. In other words: ask others for advice. 'There is an inherent limit for each of us regarding what we can know and our ability to have an objective perspective on any given situation. Yet, we can exponentially expand our knowledge and perspective by cultivating and connecting with a network of peers and colleagues – each with their own set of experiences and perspectives,' they add.[121] And this doesn't only apply when we're in crisis or overwhelm.

I know many leaders and thought leaders who struggle to do this as effectively as they could. They figure, consciously or not, that they are in the position that they are in because they know the answers and don't have to ask for others' advice. Yet, in another counter-intuitive research finding, Jonah Berger found that asking for advice not only helps us to garner useful insights, but it makes us seem smarter as well. As he reminds us, people like feeling smart.[122] They like to think that other people view them as intelligent and appreciate them for the valuable things that they have to say. So, instead of the other person thinking that we're incapable or incompetent for asking something, those who are pressed for advice tend to draw a rather different conclusion: with their pre-existing belief that their opinions are valuable, they judge us instead as smart for asking them.

Think of it as a more sophisticated version of flattery. Where flattery can look overt and obvious, and can come across as self-serving, asking for advice is more subtle, and often more effective. 'Rather than telling someone they're great, asking them for advice shows that you hold them in high regard,' Berger adds.[123] By asking for someone's advice, you're indirectly reinforcing that you think they are smart, and showing that you value their opinion. This increases the positive feelings of the advice-giver – helping them feel smarter and more confident. It also encourages them to see the people who are asking them for advice more positively as well. All of this helps in the realm of ideas and thought leadership; give your audience or followers a little more credit and they're likely to extend the same back to you.

There are no limits to the ways that you can approach asking others for advice. I've seen people engage their followers on social media via polls or through well-worded content that poses a question. Another idea could be to set up a podcast-style interview series and ask experts along to share their views on a topic.

The Antidote by Oliver Burkeman is built on Burkeman's travels through what he refers to as the 'backwards law' of negative thinking. Following several years' reporting on the field of psychology as a journalist, Burkeman started to see a pattern: the thing that united the psychologists and philosophers (and the occasional self-help guru) that he talked to was the idea that 'the effort to try to feel happy is often precisely the thing that makes us miserable'.[124] The book itself outlines Burkeman's experiences researching and asking various groups what they believe about happiness. While Burkeman states some of his own thinking in the book, it's been pulled together on the basis of perspectives from the likes of Stoics, Buddhists, the people of Mexico celebrating *el Día de los Muertos* (the Day of the Dead), and others he calls 'professional pessimists'. *The Antidote* demonstrates that a journalistic approach – committed, as the good ones are, to objectivity, balance, data gathering and interviewing – can be a good model for a more consultative style of thinking and thought leadership.

Asking questions is incredibly powerful. Go beyond the standard "What do you think?" with specific questions like:

- Where are the holes in this idea for you? What aspects of this do I need to explain better?
- What haven't I thought about or considered?
- What gets you excited about this idea?
- Can you see any evidence of bias or assumptions in this idea?
- What would you do or think in my position?
- What possibilities do you see as a result of this idea?
- Who do you think this would be most useful for?
- Are there any aspects of this idea that you disagree with? Can you help me understand what they are, and why?

When we have an open conversation, and are prepared to suspend our judgement as we listen, we welcome different viewpoints. Do this well, and your thinking becomes more inclusive. Do this even better by being proactive about seeking out opposing views. Just make sure you bring an open mind to each encounter. As Grant reminds us in *Think Again:* 'If we approach an argument as a war, there will be winners and losers. If we see it more as a dance, we can begin to choreograph a way forward.'[125]

2. Leave some aspects of your thinking unfinished or unresolved

There's another, potentially less direct way that a consultative style invites others to engage more deeply with our ideas. Authors and movie-makers use the drama inherent in conflict to keep us reading and watching because they know that conflict seizes our attention and motivates us to learn more.[126] Similarly, when we encounter questions, or something that has been left unresolved, we are more attentive and participative – whether we've been directly invited to participate or not. The very human and virtually universal reason for this is that our brain doesn't take too kindly to the unknown, unfinished and unresolved. It likes neat and tidy answers, with comprehensible things wrapped up in a pretty package and tied with string. Think about the power that's created by a dramatic cliffhanger that leaves us anticipating the next episode or instalment. We want to come back and see how the difficult situation or shock revelation is later resolved.

Similarly, when we communicate we act on the assumption that basic rules will be upheld – for example, that questions will be answered or that information that's provided will be full and complete. It's disruptive, then, when we encounter examples of these rules not being followed. Our brains are triggered to engage in more extensive processing, because we still want things to make sense. We increase our mental efforts in order to create a coherent interpretation of what is being communicated.[127] In other words, we become more invested because we're motivated to try to resolve the ambiguity and to fill in things that might have been left unsaid, or that are still not answered or solved.

This additional investment dovetails with something called the Zeigarnik Effect. Long aware of the toll and the discomfort that underlying cognitive tension has on our minds, psychologists named the experience of being able to better recall, and recall in more detail, interrupted or incomplete tasks. Imagine you're on your way to completing the last task that you were trying to get done before running out the door for school pick up, and you get interrupted by a phone call. You're frustrated that the task remains unfinished, and are wishing you'd just left the phone ringing. As a result, you carry the task home with you – not deliberately, but it seems to have lodged itself in your mind. You find yourself ruminating about it when you are stirring the dinner, and then you wake up during the night, plagued with thoughts about your next steps, despite the fact that you're not remotely prepared to solve it at that hour. The same goes when you manage to break the Netflix-binge, despite a cliffhanger or, not too long ago, when you had to wait a week for the next episode of the series to be released. In the intervening time, you replay the tense scenario that the last episode wrapped up on, and spend (sometimes far too much) mental energy wondering how the plot might go from here.

I often experienced this feeling – of taking what I had left unresolved with me – when I was writing this book. I would leave a section or chapter unfinished at the end of a writing session. I might have had a concept that was tangling me, or uncertainty about what I was trying to say or how I would stitch a particular point together. I'd go away from it because I had to attend to my family, or because I was frustrated about feeling blocked and couldn't do any more at that point. However, more often than not, my mind was still working on it. I'd wake up in the morning with clarity that I had previously lacked, or I would find that I had new sentences seemingly writing themselves in my head. The way forward suddenly looked much clearer.

It was similar when I consulted with others. I gained greater clarity as I talked about where my thinking currently was, or what I was getting tangled in, and heard how others were interpreting my conclusions or my dilemmas. Those conversational partners engaged with my ideas much more in these discussions than if I had simply been lecturing at them about the conclusions I'd reached, because I gave them a way in, an invitation to help, and to be part of solving something. They usually followed up with me later, too, because they had become more engaged with my ideas. Hearing my thinking paraphrased back to me in somebody else's words, and with their perspective added into the mix, almost always proved valuable. With this tiny bit more distance, and a different vantage point that came when I was in the role of hearing it as opposed to saying it, I could see what was missing, where people had misunderstood me and what I needed to work on because it still appeared confusing or misleading.

Play with the suspense of the unresolved or unfinished in your own work and thinking, and in the way that you share your ideas with others. Ask those you trust, or your wider network, about the parts that you haven't cracked yet as a way to get them involved in what you're doing and enhancing your thinking at the same time. You are always trying things out, but this need not be solely a solo exercise.

3. Create a community

Now that you understand the importance of enlisting others in helping you develop your thinking, you'll want to think about where you can find them, and where you can congregate them.

You'll have people that are part of the work that you are already doing, such as the clients you help, advocates or referrers, contractors or employees, suppliers or partners. Chances are you are communicating and collaborating with these people organically already, as and when is needed in the course of the work that you do. The other consideration, however, is to build a community around your thinking and ideas themselves. These people, too, will amplify your thought leadership.

You can't really build thought leadership without an audience. Sure, you can do the thinking – developing your ideas, turning them into offerings and trying them out on clients – but the leading part depends on your ability to aggregate followers around ideas and to influence, educate, and inspire. If you're wanting to go beyond the work that you're already doing and the impact that you're already having, then you need people beyond those you're currently working with to embrace your ideas, learn from you and be motivated by your expertise and thinking.

The people who are engaging with your work first-hand are the starting point for your community, but you can also go much wider. Your thought leadership community can include anyone who could benefit from your ideas. Anyone who perceives your thinking to have value or who is keen to hear what you have to say. Building an audience is about connection; it requires establishing genuine connections with people who may have never met you, but who are willing to listen to you, engage with you and potentially support you. Some of these people will find you if you're putting value out into the world, but you'll fast-track your community-building if you also put yourself out there and start reaching out. You might look for prospects, or those you could work with directly in time, but your community need not only be comprised of the ideal target audience for your offerings. Don't overlook others in parallel or complementary industries, including people with a similar target market to you. It could be the case that the value you provide, or the things you are helping people with, may also enhance goals or outcomes that they are trying to achieve.

One of the biggest mistakes that people make is trying to appeal to everybody. The more specific you are about who you exist for, the easier it is to connect with and give value to those people. Think about who your thinking is likely to have the biggest impact on, or who has a problem that can be solved with your ideas. I said before that, at whatever decibel, considered and generous thought leadership is a powerful contribution, and that's a good reminder here. It's not so much about the size of your audience, but the kind of engagement they have with what you are saying. You're much better off having a smaller group of people who are excited about your ideas – and want to talk to and learn from you – than a whole bunch of people who aren't really bothered. Especially as you want your community to be a source of conversations.

Where you build your community is far less important than the fact that you have one. Many of the aspiring thought leaders I talk to spend a lot of time thinking about, or analysing, what the right platform to be on is. It does pay to be strategic, but there's no sense in agonising over this. You can't predict all the future trends to come in communications and social platforms, so pick one or a few where you know your community will be, and start building.

One word of caution: the data on social media networks is not actually yours. These sites are a good way to gain reach, and they undoubtedly have some useful functionality for communicating, but you are beholden to those platforms' often fickle algorithms. My advice is to make the most of them – utilising what they do well – but ideally rely on social networks as only a part of your tactics. Make sure that you have another channel, like an email database, that you control and own.

From direct outreach, to commenting on others' content, providing resources, running webinars, or getting involved in other relevant conversations that are already taking place, there are countless ways that you can build your community – and these ideas reflect tactics that are done solely in the online space. Many of our clients also work with people in workshop settings, or via speaking engagements. Both are opportunities to involve others in their thinking. Still others do focus-group-style discussions or set up an informal "brains trust" for eliciting feedback and furthering their ideas.

We also encourage the use of value exchanges, a framework that we encountered when working with Greg Burgoyne from the Course Creators Academy. A value exchange is a structured conversation whereby you ask specific questions of someone in your target audience to elicit insights that are valuable to you, in exchange for giving a resource or similar that's of value to them. Mechanisms like this help you to uncover more valuable insights about your audience, shift assumptions that you're holding, and understand more fully – in your community's words – what they already think and know about your topic, as well as possible objections to your ideas or approach. (I've included a step-by-step process for a value exchange, adapted from Greg's teachings, in Chapter 9.) You may do some combination of these engagement activities. Your community-building strategy will be unique to the work that you are doing and goals around impact that you want to achieve.

Building a community requires sustained efforts to show up and provide value, but it's an important foundation for your thought leadership. You have to have something to say, but you also have to be prepared to listen; the focus is on conversations much more than just content. This is reassuring for those among us who don't want to be the loudest foghorn. Ask questions in your content that encourage others to think, and make sure that you always respond to comments. Finding and nurturing an audience means you'll have supporters of your ideas who will help your thinking to keep developing.

Our ideas go through many iterations; our Intelligent Idea Cycle suggests that you will ideate, validate, communicate and then activate your ideas, and, at every point throughout this evolution you are ideally seeking and integrating feedback to make your ideas better. The Intelligent Idea Cycle itself was subject to that same iteration. Originally it had only three stages and then, following feedback from our community, we expanded it to allow for the Ideate step to be included.

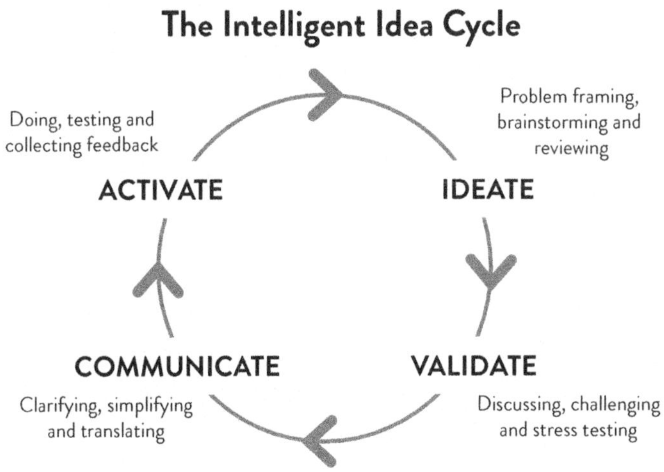

And that's just it: If you've done the work of building a community, there will be people there to listen to what you've got to say, engage and interact with your ideas, and further challenge your expertise and expand your thinking. And that's what you're here for, after all.

So far:

Encouraging and inspiring others is a key part of leadership, and an important aspect in thought leadership. Thought leadership isn't a one-way sermon delivered from your literal or symbolic stage – instead, it should be a conversation that leaves space for others to pitch in.

When you present with less certainty and ask questions, you leave room for others and inspire their thinking, engagement, and buy-in. This not only lowers the barriers for you to get started, but also enables you to reap the benefits of input from others.

To authentically lean into a consultative style in service of better:

- Increase your comfort in collaboration, by directly asking for others' advice and contributions.
- Leave aspects of your thinking unresolved, or your ideas unfinished in order to invite others to participate.
- Create a community of people to have conversations with. You will provide value in communicating with them and they will help you to extend your thinking and ideas.

CHAPTER 8

Allowing our thinking to evolve

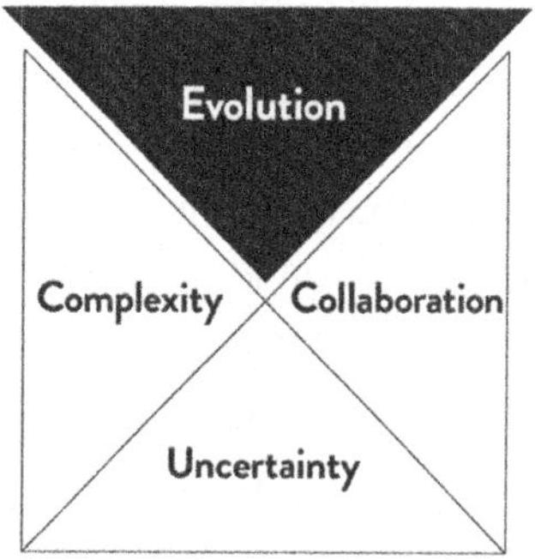

In the introduction to *Effortless: Make It Easier to Do What Matters Most*, Greg McKeown includes a confession. Under the subheading 'The Dilemma', McKeown outlines the challenge that he was having with his own ideas. He was striving to model Essentialism, an idea espoused in his earlier work *Essentialism: The Disciplined Pursuit of Less.*

He was being as selective as he had ever been, stripping away the non-essentials, taking a break from teaching, and resisting the urge to write a new book. But it still felt too much. McKeown admits:

> I could feel the cracks in an assumption I had always held to: that to achieve everything we want without becoming impossibly busy or overextended, we simply need to discipline ourselves to only say "yes" to essential activities and "no" to everything else. But now I found myself wondering: what does one do when they've stripped life down to the essentials and it's *still* too much?[128]

He goes on to explain his brush with burnout and the self-imposed pressure he felt to be the perfect Essentialist. As he bounces back up from the bottom, he shares what he learnt: 'I was doing the right things for the right reasons. But I was doing them in the wrong way.' And this is how he positions his new book to build on and extend the previous one. '*Essentialism* was about doing the right things; *Effortless* is about doing them in the right way'.[129] He goes on to connect the need for this to what so many of us are feeling. As a reader, I could relate, and I felt the urgency of what he was promising next. It was powerful. I was absolutely hooked and hanging onto his every word as he shared a whole new way that we could choose to work and live.

This provided a stark realisation for me. Far from losing trust in him because his original thinking didn't solve all that it had promised to, I gained respect for the fact that he had fronted up and offered more. In explicitly stating the limitations of what he had been thinking until then, and showing me how he was going to update it, I felt like he was taking me on the journey. I was right there ready to learn and evolve with him.

I had a similar experience when I was researching this book and read Thomas Curran's *The Perfection Trap*. Ironically, gripped as he is by perfectionism, Curran admits how he had grown to dislike the title and focus of his earlier TED Talk. Despite being proud to have done a presentation of that nature, Curran claims that the talk is far too personal, wrongly placing the onus on individuals for their perfectionism, when there are actually much larger and more pervasive forces at play. Curran explains how:

> Writing this book – buried in that tricky art of collecting thoughts in neat little sentences, then tweaking and distilling them into something plain for others to read – has been clarifying. Through it, I've found gaps in my thinking that I didn't know existed. And I've started to see things in the data and all around me, things I'd somehow missed or simply couldn't see.[130]

Like McKeown, he's effectively discrediting some of his earlier work, but he's doing so in a way that then takes us further.

•••

When you're pushing somewhere new or better, it's always going to be about iteration and refinement. This can be a disheartening aspect of thought leadership, thinking, or growth in general. But it's also an exciting one, if we can embrace and accept the idea, as opposed to that feeling of "not finished" putting us off starting or sharing where we are along the way.

I've seen the fear that it's not done enough or ready yet deter many aspiring thought leaders, or detain would-be authors. And I get it. When you're putting something out there, it (and you, by extension) are subject to judgement. For a book, the stakes feel especially high. A book is a very tangible and fixed (once it's printed) representation of someone's ideas. You absolutely should evolve that to get it as robust and insightful as it can be. Yet, if you ever want it to be out in the world, you can't tinker and tweak it indefinitely – tempting as that is. I thought I had reached the finish-line many times with this book before I actually was ready to hand it over for typesetting – and one of our other participants in the Better Book Project described his long titivating stage as being akin to tidying or 'rearranging the deck chairs on the Titanic.' Eventually, though, we need to let things go and send our book to print. One of the things that I often remind authors of at this stage – and have had to have stern words about with myself a few times – is that letting your work go out into the world does not preclude you from being able to comment any further on that topic in future.

As McKeown's example attests, we can still update our thinking – either through another edition of our existing book, or by building out our concepts further as we choose what to write next. If people can overcome the continual rework loop with their books, then you can do it with other ways you're sharing your ideas, too – whether that be the social content you are putting out there, videos you're filming, or a keynote you are getting ready to deliver. Our ideas are made to continually evolve and improve. However, just because they are going to still mature further, doesn't mean they don't have value as they are now, too.

We don't need to have everything figured out and undoubtedly right before we take it out into the world. And while this is absolutely not an excuse for shoddy thinking, or flouting fact-checking, testing and evidence, it is an invitation to let go of any illusion of a necessary endpoint. Because as well as not wanting oversimplified arguments, we do want evolving ones.

By now we've explored the importance of complex arguments, and we know that it's vital that we're able to change our minds. We've seen the power of uncertainty and learnt how leaving some aspects unsolved can increase collaboration and engagement. All of this sets the stage for evolving our thinking. Changing our minds, however, can be hard.

Understanding the brain provides some clues as to why. If uncertainty or unresolved information is threatening, then it's natural to want to hold tight to our established (and comfortable) views, even as we come into contact with evidence to the contrary. That's our default setting, at least as far as the path of least resistance is concerned. If we're not careful – and diligent about doing better – we have a tendency to resist new information and persevere with our initial beliefs. Sometimes even when we're aware of the need to be open to new evidence or insights, the temptation towards hard-headedness is alluring.

Research suggests that we're more likely to change our minds when we can do so privately, as opposed to publicly, which backs up the lived experience of many of us that it's hard to outwardly admit that we were wrong.[131] It's hard to admit errors to ourselves, but we especially don't want to be seen as flaky or previously ill-informed by others. We don't want to risk undermining what we've said before, and we fear that we will diminish the trust that we've worked hard to earn from others if we go back on or revise something we've previously asserted. However logical this fear seems, my Greg McKeown example demonstrates that this outcome isn't always what occurs.

Other research also backs this up. In researching an article for her award-winning blog *The Leaders Digest*, Suzi McAlpine was reflecting on research from Martha Jeong, Leslie K. John, Francesca Gino and Laura Huang around how leaders are actually perceived as less intelligent if they don't ever shift their thinking.[132] Add to that the other problems that we encounter when we become too entrenched – less listening, less learning, poorer decisions, and coming across as arrogant and rigid – and it's a nasty combination that we'd all do well to avoid.

To determine what others think of those who refuse to change their minds, and in particular how leaders who fail to do so are perceived, Jeong and her colleagues set up a series of experiments. First, they replicated a similar study to that by the European researchers that we heard about in Chapter 6. They looked at the outcome of entrepreneurs – typically prized for their confidence – refusing to change their mind in a pitch competition. They found that 76 percent of entrepreneurs dug in their heels, even in the face of contradictory evidence. And they also found that, despite popular logic or pressure that suggests that being steadfast and bold is best, this approach didn't pay off for them. The entrepreneurs who were able to change their minds during the pitch were almost six times more likely to advance to the final round of the competition. This was in line with the favourable findings for the "scientific-thinking" group that we saw in that earlier study. We know that the real-life rewards in terms of revenue also favoured those who were more flexible in that exercise. What the latter study revealed, however, that the earlier study didn't, was that it enhances others' perceptions of us when we're able to evolve our thinking.

Further research by Jeong and her colleagues elaborates on why this is the case. In a follow-up experiment that saw participants play the role of investors appraising entrepreneurs, they found that people perceived those who changed their minds as lacking confidence but demonstrating greater intelligence. Unsurprisingly, how we feel about others changing their minds depends on the context. In some settings we might disparage others for equivocating, whereas in other situations we applaud them for their thoughtfulness. We also feel differently based on how (and if) we have been directly impacted by the outcomes of others' ideas or their changed minds.

However, when it comes to the information and conversations happening out there in our collective ideascape, we need to err on the side of evolving. We don't want to flip-flop constantly, nor be blown around on the winds of popular opinion with no conviction of our own, but we need to avoid the damage that can be done when we get too dug-in and won't move our mindsets. Changing our mind doesn't have to be about turning 180 degrees; it can be smaller tweaks and iterations as we come to do more and know more.

Our thinking should start from the solid foundation of experience and expertise that we have established, but always and continuously build from there. This is where Grant's description of confident humility that we explored in Chapter 6, comes in handy. That balance of belief that we will still get to better outcomes and that we're capable of moving closer towards mastery, while showing flexibility and acknowledging gaps or errors in our thinking.[133]

Although hard, changing our minds makes our thinking and outcomes better

Rigid thinking is unproductive. With the pace of change and increasing complexity, and in light of how much new information we receive, we're being forced to rethink constantly. Not only does the best thinking rely on us continually revisiting and updating our views, but good leadership requires it also – and those are the two ingredients we're looking to bring together here.

When we are rigid against evolving and improving our thinking, we remain fixed in the mindset that we're more naturally predisposed to. We need people with different perspectives, different lenses, different ways of processing information, different risk profiles. We need diverse thinking, as we have seen.

In Chapter 1, we saw the 2008 Wall Street collapse as an example of what happens when one dominant approach reigns supreme. The story showed, with startling clarity, the devastating consequences of getting too dug-in and refusing to shift our thinking and behaviour. Those who held the greatest power didn't allow their minds, nor their actions, to be changed. They were not open to letting their thinking evolve or improve. Although it had dire consequences, this example highlights the power of our ideas and thinking. It demonstrates a dramatic and easily observable consequence of allowing only one type of person to be talking, and of what can happen when we choose to listen to, and base our behaviour on, only one type of thinking. Or when we try to eradicate or over-rule uncertainty and doubt.

The best people to lead our thinking, and influence our behaviours, hold their views a little more lightly than that. They are flexible about what they know. They are humble. They adapt their thinking when new information comes to light. And they invite new information in – not seeing it as undermining their position, but instead for its ability to enhance their position. They value what they can learn from others. But this takes work.

Most of us take pride in our knowledge and expertise, and we form a large part of our identities around what we think, know, and stand for. We often value our ability to stay true to our beliefs and opinions. And this makes sense in a stable world. Yet most of us understand that we live in anything but a stable world. The result is that we need to spend as much time rethinking as we do thinking. Changing our minds helps us to be seen as more intelligent, flexible, open-minded, and willing to learn and grow – all of which strengthens our ability to lead ourselves and to lead others.

Research also suggests that the ability to change our minds helps us to arrive at better answers, too.[134] While there's some logic to this – if we assimilate more learning, we know more and surely have a higher chance to landing closer to the mark – it actually goes against some of our deeply-held ideas and behaviours as they relate to our intuition and instincts. We more commonly think our first answer is correct.

Think about the last time you took a multiple-choice test.

Imagine you have filled in all your answers, and find yourself sitting there with additional time. You start scanning your sheet to see whether there were any answers that you feel less sure about. The majority of students are convinced that if they change away from their initial answer, they are more likely to go from a right answer to a wrong one, as opposed to changing a wrong answer into the correct one. They trust their gut instincts or automatic responses more than their ability to reason towards something better, so they fear that revising their answer is more likely to hurt their score. This phenomenon is known as the "first-instinct fallacy". And it's a fallacy because the truth actually goes in the other direction. 'When a trio of psychologists conducted a comprehensive review of thirty-three studies, they found that in every one, the majority of answer revisions were from wrong to right,' Grant shares.[135] Part of this could, of course, be that because people are so hesitant to rethink their answers, they only make changes when they are fairly confident – but regardless, the evidence suggests that those who do rethink, rather than staying anchored to their first answers, tend to improve their scores.

How can you do this better?

I like to think of rethinking or unlearning as the pulling back of a slingshot that is needed in order to launch an object. It creates tension, and it can feel like a backwards step, but it's ultimately what propels us forward.

Amy Edmondson, Professor of Leadership at Harvard Business School, distinguishes between three different types of failure in *Right Kind of Wrong: Why Learning to Fail Can Teach*

Us to Thrive. These are basic, complex and intelligent failures, and all of them spur different learning. While basic failures have a single cause (and it's often human error), complex failures result from the perfect storm of multiple factors lining up in the wrong way. The third type, intelligent failures, are the result of experiments into new territory – those that occur when we are making progress or discoveries. When we are consciously working to learn. This is the type of so-called failure that we should be pursuing. As well as taking place in new and previously unexplored territory, intelligent failures occur when we're in pursuit of a valued goal, and they happen despite adequate preparation and risk mitigation. They take place when the answers are unknowable in advance. Trying a radically new method or model, designing an innovative product, or testing reactions in a brand-new market are all activities that require intelligent failures if we hope to make progress and succeed. Learning is necessary, and a good sign here.

We all have the ability to learn and to actively evolve our thinking – we just need to exercise it. In order to authentically allow your thinking to evolve in service of better, you'll need to make the required effort to integrate new information that you learn, embrace where you've come from while you grow and evolve, and draw on your courage to release your thinking before it might feel totally ready.

1. Assimilate and accommodate new information

Swiss psychologist Jean Piaget's Cognitive Development Theory outlines a couple of ways by which we meet new information, and evolve and improve our thinking.[136] The first is by assimilating new information into our existing cognitive structures – the aforementioned schema.

Assimilation occurs when we encounter new information that aligns relatively well with what we already think, information that reinforces and strengthens our current understanding of the world. Unsurprisingly, it's not overly difficult, discomforting or cognitively demanding to integrate this new information into our pre-existing mental frameworks. It doesn't require too much shifting or changing on our part. Assimilation, in other words, is relatively effortless.

What does require much more effort is accommodation, which is what we're forced to do when we encounter new evidence or experiences that don't neatly fit in with our existing schema, ideas or beliefs. With assimilation we are called on to modify or expand our existing cognitive structures based on new information. As you will know from encountering someone with radically opposite political views, or a very different stance on a contentious issue, this can be challenging and confronting. It requires much more work from us, too; we have to actively adapt and refine our mental frameworks. Much like our openness to new ideas, and like we saw in practising learning new things in Chapter 6, accommodation is a skill that gets better the more that we do it.

Absolutely we can practise disciplined curiosity as we saw in Chapter 5. We can approach new knowledge as a scientist might as we learnt more about in Chapter 6. And we can expand our knowledge base and evolve our ideas by asking for other perspectives as we explored in Chapter 7. Another powerful way to encounter additional information and evolve what you know is in deepening your experience and expanding your evidence base.

Continuing to try out what you're thinking in the course

of your work – to test your theories and assumptions – helps you to update your thinking. Run more experiments, and expand the community that you are working with, even if that means you ask for volunteers for lower-rate or pro-bono offerings that enable you to gather knowledge more quickly. We've looked already at the edge that practising professionals have as thought leaders, and this is part of the reason why. There's a virtuous cycle that comes when you are elbows-deep in doing the thing that you do; you have a ripe testing ground for trialling your thinking. Results and feedback from those tests then assimilate back in, provided you have built-in some reflection and feedback loops, as our next section explores. Stay curious about the results you are getting. And ask questions of the people you are working with, especially where you think you might be acting on an assumption.

2. Embrace your earlier efforts as part of your evolution

On some level, most of us know that our knowledge is constantly evolving and our expertise is continually deepening (at least as far as we proactively work at, or try to get better at, something). Most of us don't own that publicly, though, or show the progress. Doing so is a lesson in – and demonstration of – humility. While sometimes there's a noticeable shift we need to make or can feel ourselves making to evolve our thinking (as is the case with accommodation), there's also the more subtle and simple passage of time that moves our ideas forward and matures them. Our thinking shifts and evolves in almost imperceptible ways each day, especially as we engage in assimilation.

It's a bit like a child growing. If we see them every day, we don't generally notice them getting any taller. It's only when we visit a child after not seeing them for a time, or when we look back at photos (or have them try on a pair of pants from the previous season or year), that we can clearly see the growth that's occurred. We don't notice it happening in the little ways.

The same goes for the small but significant shifts happening in our minds. It's common not to notice or feel our thinking changing until we're confronted with something from some time ago. We're then quick to be embarrassed by our earlier efforts or examples of our thinking. Think of the way you cringe when someone says they checked out your website, especially if you know full well that the content that you have on there was written years ago. Chances are high that it no longer really reflects or does justice to what you do now. Or consider how you feel if you look back on a video you filmed five years ago. Aside from admiring your youthful glow, or potentially chuckling about a bad haircut, it's totally normal to think 'Ugh – what on Earth …?' about what you are saying, too.

I see this with aspiring authors also. One had written some of the content for her book a year earlier, and then set it aside. When she sent it through, she expected that I would be able to pick up the 30,000 words that she had then, and take it further towards the finish-line. It was quickly obvious however, in the conversations I had with her that would enable me to ghost-write the rest of it, that her thinking had moved on as a result of the work she had been doing since then. Most of what she had already written needed significant reworking to bring it up to speed before I could build out the rest.

As a business, we have also encountered this when we experimented with an idea for social content. Realising that we had more than a decade of articles in our website's blog archives that virtually no-one looked at, but which still had some valuable thinking, we decided to share one every couple of weeks with a new blurb. The first few articles that were selected by the team were genuinely cringe-worthy. I looked at our 2013 take on LinkedIn, and suddenly felt like a dinosaur. A reflection of the times, sure, but it certainly hadn't aged well. The world, and we, had come a long way in our understanding since then.

My instant reaction was to backtrack. 'Before you share this, we need to edit and update it; we certainly don't want to draw attention to these ideas how they are currently,' I asserted. But then I caught myself and stopped. I thought about the advice I would give, and that I had actually recently given to a client. I had encouraged her to leave her original article as it was and use the blurb to humbly highlight how her thinking had moved on and changed. Perhaps we could do the same? I leaned into the discomfort and swallowed a sip of my own medicine. The idea of #IntelligentRethink was born.

The tendency, when new information comes to light, is to backfill, and remove any trace that we ever didn't have this additional part in our understanding. We rush to assimilate (or sometimes accommodate) the updated insights as though we had known them all along. We use our pre-existing thinking as the frame to help us organise and categorise the new stuff, and then build that in. Our brains want to help us maintain our sense of coherence in how we understand the world, which is fine, and often helpful. When we cover up the continually evolving nature of our thinking, however, we lose the opportunity to demonstrate our growth. Resist this urge, and instead pause and acknowledge the journey.

Show the movement and progress you've made. Not only

do you not need to be afraid to change your view, but you can also show where you might have fallen short in your thinking previously and then take people with you. Just like I urged you to show the scope of what you know and what you don't, you can outwardly admit to what you used to think, and what you believe to be true now. It can be nostalgic and endearing to bump into what we used to think, and it can be humorous for readers, too. It shows transparent humility and engenders trust, like in the Greg McKeown example that opened this chapter. In publicly examining our thinking, we are demonstrating a willingness to move on, to grow.

I personally put more stock in what someone is saying when they have shown me that their reflection and learning loops are robust. It firms up what they are saying today as well as showing courage and great leadership.

3. Set it free

If we know that we're never actually finished with our thinking or idea, it can be tricky to know when you, or your thinking, is ready to go out into the world. With no clear end point, there's the potential for endless thinking or over-thinking. There comes a point, however, when you need to let things go and allow them to be tested out. Of course scientists hope their hypotheses are right, but they have to move past just thinking about it and try things out to know for sure. It's estimated that experiments fail 95 percent of the time, but scientists are able to string multiple experiments together to progress towards their goals. They know that while a bias for action can get them started, progress requires iteration.

Our Roadmapping Your Reputation workshop wasn't anywhere near finished before we sold it. In fact, we sold it to two clients (at introductory pricing) before we were even sure what the output would look like. However, we knew the value that we were going to deliver via the workshop, and were able to communicate that to the initial prospects that we knew it could have a big impact for. We bit the bullet and started to share it.

In doing so, we learnt a couple of key lessons. We learnt that when you've got a deadline, you'll be forced to figure stuff out. We also learnt that being under that kind of pressure is when you learn the most. Only in doing those first couple of workshops were we able to work out what the deliverable afterwards should consistently be. We could have spun our wheels and speculated endlessly, but instead we had to put a first cut of it together to present to those who had paid for it. And we absolutely delivered value. From there, we received feedback that told us what we still needed to work on and some of the ways that we could improve both the offering and the output.

A few years on, Roadmapping Your Reputation is a robust framework that helps our clients pinpoint their strategic thought leadership positioning and create a solid plan for moving from experienced expert to trusted authority. It has provided dozens of people and organisations with a thought leadership toolkit and the building blocks to leverage their position. Undoubtedly, it has taken us a while to get it to this point, but it wouldn't have happened if we hadn't started using and testing it. If we hadn't enlisted others to help us improve it.

If you're seeing success with your current clients, bringing value and moving them towards better outcomes – as shown by retaining your clients, receiving referrals, and sustaining a commercial endeavour – then you have something worth venturing. If a small number of people are already benefitting from what you do, in the way that you do it, then it's safe to say that others will, too, as you increase your impact – especially if you've done the work to establish and identify your target audience, and you understand the problem you solve or the challenge you alleviate for them. If you don't look back on your earlier efforts and cringe at least a little, then you waited too long to release something. We should be evolving, and that knowledge can be an empowering frame from which to start.

Think about the ideas and thinking – the unique approaches, methodologies or frameworks – that you are sitting on and where you can pursue a win–win with those.

As self-professed changemaker Beth Comstock says,

> New ideas and observations are far from perfect on their day of birth. Often, you can't even put the concept into words. That's why I firmly believe in running a fitness test for them – and those tests require a place where people feel free to speak, make mistakes, argue and iterate.[137]

Let it go, and make it safe to engage with what you are trying. Your thinking will benefit from being set free and allowed to evolve with others, but you'll also be bringing clients value, or using your expertise to help them solve their problems. In letting your ideas out there, even if you are forced to figure it out further as you go, you will discover that you know far more than you think you do.

So far:

Although you need to have your ideas and thinking in a place where they have value and are ready to share, you will still – and always – continue learning. Sometimes that may even see you rethinking significantly or changing your mind.

We can be solid in our position, while still holding our views lightly. Allowing your thinking to develop and evolve – and including others on that journey – is a powerful way to build trust and encourage others to rethink and learn more also.

To authentically allow your thinking to evolve in service of better:

- integrate and assimilate new information that you learn – even when this isn't easy, you need to allow your ideas to be updated
- outwardly own and embrace your earlier efforts – show where you've come from while you learn more, grow and evolve, and
- set your ideas and expertise free, sometimes even before they feel totally ready – trusting that this is the best way to review and refine them.

CHAPTER 9

It's time to do something

Learning is fantastic. Eventually, however, you have to actually get up and do something. As the author of *Atomic Habits* James Clear reminds us: 'Life rewards action, not intelligence.'[138]

It's common for brilliant people to talk themselves out of getting started. I see this reluctance all the time, whether in procrasti-learning or other, more overt, avoidance tactics. It's what has spurred me to write this book, after all. And while I appreciate the time and energy you have put into reading it, and to expanding your perspective about thought leadership as a vehicle for greater impact, it will have been for nothing if you don't then use your increased understanding and confidence to take action.

I'm currently helping Grant Baker, a successful businessman and investor, to tell his story. His journey includes several high-profile partnerships and multiple

$100-million-plus business exits and sales. He's got every reason to be out there swinging; however, Grant is modest and self-effacing about how he got started. In our conversations he has shared how he was relatively late to the game of being in business for himself, and has described his naïveté when he finally did take the plunge at the age of 35. Grant admits that if he had known more, he might not have done it – while attesting that sometimes it's best not to know too much. This was a lesson cemented by Grant's uncle, a nuclear physicist. 'I remember him telling me that he would never be any good at business because he knew too much. He believed he would always be able to work out a reason not to do anything,' Grant laughed. This is why we see so many incredible and smart people falter far before the finish-line, or even before they've really begun to run the race.

Now that you've seen a wider-ranging and more inclusive span of what can work, and you've increased your understanding of what better can look like, it's time for you to take action towards your vision for better. This chapter will help you to start stepping into your authentic version of thought leadership in order to increase the impact of your ideas and realise their potential, even if it still feels scary. Let's see how.

1. Start with a clear and fiery foundation

Being smart doesn't necessarily help with having the courage to act. It's impossible to have an impact if you're not doing anything, though, so you do need to find a way to get in the game. In Chapter 3 we talked about getting a right-sized grounding of genuine confidence in your expertise and the value you have to offer. We also saw that those who truly make an impact – who are compelled to do something – are fuelled by a fire they can't ignore. Now is the time to not only find your fire, but direct it towards action. It's not enough just to have a wild and well-meaning hope that something could get better; you need to be clear about how you will make it so.

At Intelligent Ink, when we start the journey of building thought leadership with our passionate and purpose-led clients, we get them to start with a clear vision of what better looks like – both for themselves, and for others. Chances are that you have similarly strong beliefs that fuel what you are doing. You know what you stand for and are working to improve. The first stage, then, is to shape your conviction that something could be better into a concrete vision.

Ask yourself (and get specific about):

- What is the change or improvement I am seeking to make? How do I want to make the world a better place?
- Why do I do what I do? What gets me out of bed in the morning?
- What's the most important or impactful thing about what I do?
- Why does that matter?

Ask yourself this last question at least five times – not to come up with similar answers, but to interrogate each of your previous answers and drill down further.

For example, our purpose at Intelligent Ink is to bring better thinking to the world. We are here to help more of the ideas, perspectives, frameworks and strategies that can make things better for people to reach the people who need them.

To arrive at that, we followed a "Why" journey that loosely looked like this:

What is the most important or impactful thing that you do?
We help to make our clients' thinking better.

And why does it matter that our clients are thinking better?
Because then they are working with ideas that have the greatest possible chance of being effective and having a positive impact.

And why does it matter that their ideas are effective and have a positive impact?
If their ideas are effective then they'll be doing better work, meaning they have a better business. And a better business means a more sustainable business that can keep going and have an even more significant impact.

And why does it matter that they're having a more significant impact?
Because the positive ripples of that impact will mean things are getting better for even more people.

And why do we care about making things better for more people?
Because that's what they are here for. It will mean that their version of better will be happening.

We often joke that if you keep going on this exercise long enough you'll eventually get to world peace (or near offer) as a final answer. What you're looking for is a step back from that – the part that you can uniquely influence or that you're contributing to. What I've included here is for the purposes of providing an example and, while it might appear that our answers reduce things down too far to be helpful, there is a lot inferred in each answer to those of us inside the business.

Getting to the heart of things requires stripping away the extraneous. In getting clearer and more tangible about the true impact of the change you are driving, this exercise moves your purpose to becoming a deeper, fire-sparking vision, which is a powerful propellant for action.

Once you've established your "Why", ask yourself:

- What would having a bigger impact mean in terms of the change that I am trying to create with my ideas? (Dream big for this; be idealistic.)
- What does success ultimately look like – both for me, and the people I am here for – when it comes to this work?
- If I achieved my version of better, how would I feel? What would I get?
- If I continue doing what I'm doing now, and don't increase the impact of my ideas any further, what will I miss out on? How would I feel then?
- And, if I achieve my version of better, what will it mean for others? What will they get, and how are they going to feel?
- Likewise, if I continued only as I am now, without affecting any bigger impact, who would be missing out? And what exactly would they miss out on?

To answer these questions, you need some idea of who you are here for – who you are trying to improve things for. These people or groups will be further fuelling you, so it pays to wrap them into your clarity work.

As we've seen, the goal of thought leadership isn't simply to build the biggest audience that you can, but to get your ideas in front of the right people – the ones who they will have the most impact for.

Consider:

- Who can I have the most positive impact on? These could be the people you currently most enjoy working with, or who you imagine you would.
- What differentiates these ideal people from others? Remember you're not trying to bend to suit everyone, so get clear on who your target audience is not, too.
- What is the need that I am meeting specifically? Are the people you are thinking about of a particular age or life stage? Do they all reside within a similar role or industry? Do they live in a specific country?

Think about how far you want to take what you are thinking and doing:

- Do I want to be making an impact in my local community?
- Do I want to influence my industry domestically?
- Or am I aiming to take my ideas worldwide?

When you have drilled this down, think about what you know about these people.

- What do they care most about? What do they believe in?
- What are they trying to achieve that they don't currently have the tools for?
- Are they trying to attain a goal, or escape or alleviate a problem? (These are different sources of motivation.)

- What challenges are they up against?
- In what ways do my knowledge and experience help them achieve their goals or tackle their challenges?
- How would they succeed if they were able to apply what I know/do?
- What would that mean for them? What ripples would it create?
- What objections are they likely to have to my ideas?
- Where are they currently getting their information from? What are their trusted sources?

You might be able to answer some of these questions yourself – or make some good guesses – but don't underestimate the value of talking to people and hearing it directly from them. There may be people in your network already who fit the audience you've identified, or you may need to reach out more widely (e.g. on social media, or via others' networks). We encourage our clients at this point to do value exchanges, as I introduced in Chapter 7.

The idea of a value exchange is what it says on the tin: you give something of value to people in your target audience in exchange for finding out more insights about them. In the value exchange framework, you list the pain points or frustrations that you think these people might be facing – then create something that would help them alleviate that pain. It could be a checklist that helps them move forward with confidence, a self-diagnostic with tailored tips, or a quick-start guide. A client recently wanted to get a sense of pricing from her peers in the market, so she reached out to people to have an open conversation about pricing. In return, each participant received an anonymised report of how others were charging.

You'll know what's right based on the work you're doing.

While you want a value exchange to be a friendly chat far more than a sales call, structure the conversation loosely around key questions that help you towards your goals. I would also urge you not to get too bogged down or stuck at this stage; it can be another form of avoidance or procrastination – especially in those with "I need to learn/know more before I can get started" tendencies. Limit yourself. Invest a couple of weeks into talking to people, and then move forward with the information you have. You can trust that you will learn more as you keep moving forward.

2. Trust that your confidence will build as you go

There's an idea that we need to be ready before we start something new. Yet as we saw when we got to know more about our inner critic in Chapter 3, we're rarely – if ever – going to feel ready when we're setting off to do something big. Sitting and waiting for confidence before you act doesn't work, because it's in taking action that we build confidence and reduce fear.

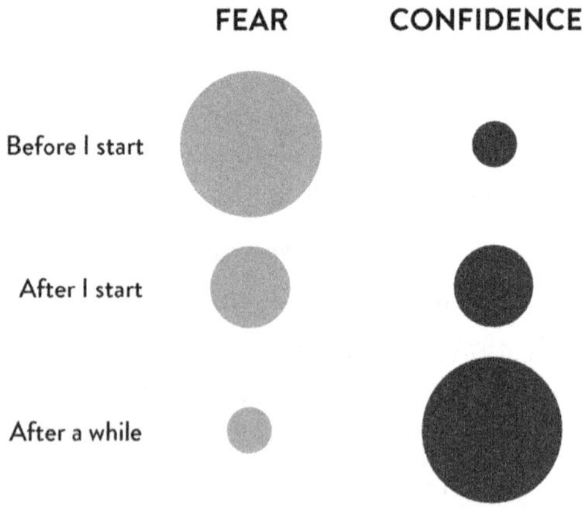

I had this experience in late 2022 when I wanted to try a new local gym. Not only was this specific gym completely new to me, but so was going to any gym at all. Yet I knew that I wanted to both keep up with, and participate in, the adventures of my three boys as they grew, so I needed something more than my current yoga regime was giving me.

Walking in that first day was scary, so I took my husband along. Knowing I had his moral support – and some practical help with exercises and machines that were all completely foreign to me – was enough to lower the stakes. It turns out I needn't have worried. The format of the training and demonstrations made it fairly foolproof, but I had to do it scared to start with. Now I know a dumbbell from a kettlebell. I can provide pointers and technique tips to other newer members. And my kids tire before I do in our games of backyard soccer. This is only the case because I started.

There's a lot written about starting before you're ready. Motivational materials abound and there are mantras to this effect in abundance. James Clear, in reflecting on an interview with Richard Branson, says that if he were to sum up the habits of successful people into just one phrase, it would be that they start before they feel ready. After hearing his story, Clear knew that Branson wasn't sitting on a panel spouting things like 'Screw it, just get on and do it!' because they sounded good. There was plenty of evidence that he was also living the approach that he preached.[139] Branson is an example of the so-called "chosen ones" who have actually chosen themselves. Backing themselves enough to start is a cornerstone of so many stories – including that of Grant Baker, who I introduced at the start of this chapter. He started before he was ready, selling his house to give him the money to invest in his first venture. Even Adam Grant, whose TED Talks have over 35 million views and who commands speaking fees ranging between US$75,000 and US$100,000 per engagement, is a self-professed shy introvert who went from being terrified of the stage to coming to *like* public speaking.[140] This was a guy who was afraid to raise his hand in class, or to answer the phone (remember that little rush of nerves in the days before caller-ID?). Yet, as a graduate student, he was determined to get over his fear of public speaking, and fast. 'I didn't have time to dip my toe in the shallow end of exposure therapy; I dove right into the deep end of flooding,' he explains, detailing how he volunteered to give a series of guest lectures in his friends' undergraduate classes.[141] The feedback was definitely not all sparkling, but over the next couple of years he went on to give more than 100 keynote speeches and many more presentations. Things started to change.

In *Hidden Potential,* Grant says that while it's unlikely there will be a day when we wake up and suddenly feel prepared, instead we become prepared by taking the leap anyway. Not only does waiting for the ideal moment mean we miss out on the benefits we'd accrue if we'd tried out our ideas, but inaction also leads to a sense of powerlessness and incompetence.[142] We get stuck in a "should" spiral and waste precious mental energy that we could be using to take us towards better.

Find your first little seeds and start planting them. Dip your toe into posting on LinkedIn. Arrange to speak through your thinking or approach with a small group. Publish a shorter ebook first. I can't tell you exactly what tactic here is going to be best for you, but do something. Either the thing, or a smaller part of it - whatever it is that will get you going.

In *Steal Like an Artist: 10 Things Nobody Told You About Being Creative*, Austin Kleon writes that it's in making things that we get to know ourselves.

> If I'd waited to know who I was or what I was about before I started "being creative", well, I'd still be sitting around trying to figure myself out instead of making things. In my experience, it's in the act of making things and doing our work that we figure out who we are.[143]

And Beth Kempton, bestselling author and writing mentor, shares a similar sentiment. If she had waited until her books were perfect, she would have never got anywhere. 'Each one has been possible because of the books that went before it,' she shares.[144]

It's true that when we're working on something important, we're never going to feel fully ready. 'A sign of doing challenging work is that you're pulled by excitement and pushed by confusion at the same time.'[145] Growth is inevitable, though, once we get started. We learn that we are ready by doing the thing – usually not just once, but over and over again. This is what builds our confidence and reduces our fear. But we have to start doing it in the first place.

3. Lower the stakes enough to get started

It's all well and good to know that we need to dive in, but quite another thing to actually take the plunge. A lofty vision can be powerful fuel for helping us move when we're underway somewhere, but it can be potentially paralysing or, at least, intimidating, when we're still trying to get started. Lowering the stakes and breaking your goal into smaller steps will help you get there. It's not about letting yourself off; you're still in pursuit of big impact, but it's okay to find a balance to help you get started.

Stakes-lowering strategy #1: View it all as an experiment

We've already seen that we can learn a lot from scientists, and it helps to lower the stakes if you approach your journey to build thought leadership as a series of experiments. Your authentic thought leadership is real, not perfect – so you don't need to aspire to perfection. Test things out. Bring a sense of playfulness and curiosity. Have a try. Be okay with some of your attempts being terrible. (They likely won't be, but it's freeing to accept that the odd disaster won't sink the ship.) If you don't take things too seriously, you're not so wedded to the outcomes.

While of course the work you are doing overall is important, none of the individual things you try matter as much as you think they do. A single LinkedIn post or article presents next to no risk in the overall scheme of things. It feels much more significant to us, because we are putting important thinking that we're closely connected to out there – but our impact is the result of the sum of all of our activity, never just a single activity.

It can also be excruciatingly uncomfortable to get up on stage to speak, or to be challenged on something you have written – but these moments are fast and fleeting. They blow past quickly and are soon forgotten. They're just one drop in the ocean of the work that you are doing to realise your vision. Viewed through this lens, even the so-called failures are tolerable. And, if we embrace the spirit of learning that we looked at in Chapter 8, those moments bring us big benefits, too. You will be refining things all the time as you go.

Kempton puts it this way: 'When we put questions out into the world and take some action without holding tight to what the result needs to be, things open up for us.'[146] If we choose not to share anything, we miss out on too much.

> The joy of connecting with others, seeing the impact of your words, allowing yourself to be seen and showing others that you see them. It's a choice that denies others the medicine you have to offer. It's a choice that denies you the reward of knowing that medicine helped someone. I promise you that, on balance, it's worth the risk.[147]

Stakes-lowering strategy #2: Take some pressure off

Downplaying the significance of each individual piece of activity creates a mindset of experimentation, and lowers the stakes in a practical way so you can move forward.

When I was writing this book, I blocked out time each week to work on the content. Sometimes, I sat down at my computer and my thinking flowed through my fingers and onto the keyboard like magic. Other times, I sat down and stared at a blank screen, absolutely convinced that I had nothing of value to say. The latter feeling was particularly present when I was pushing into slightly newer territory with my thinking.

When I was tackling topics that didn't feel so well-organised, or that I didn't feel so well-versed in, I had to lower the stakes in order to explore. Trying to come up with something brilliant that I could craft into the book felt like too much pressure at that point, so instead I would plan to just write a LinkedIn post about the idea first. I knew that it could only be 3,000 words at most, instead of the possible 60,000 or 70,000 in a full book that I could get tangled in. This helped me to distil my thinking more succinctly. Sometimes the substance of the post made it into the book, and often it didn't. Sometimes I wrote far past the end of the post, inspired by the topic I was toying with, and sometimes that post was all I got done in that writing session. I was still making progress. I was showing up, in service of my ideas, and developing them further. I was learning, too, in those moments, that I could keep going even when it was hard, and this was even more helpful for my overall confidence.

Look at where you can take away some pressure. Lower the stakes by reducing the size of what you need to deliver, the size of the audience that you start speaking to, or the scope of what you are trying to put out there. Whatever it is that allows you to start. Small progress is still progress – and that's better than nothing.

Stakes-lowering strategy #3: Balance comfort and challenge

Lowering the stakes helps us get out of our own way and take action. To grow as a thought leader, however, you're going to need to balance comfort with challenge. You're going to have to push yourself. As with many things in life, your success is going to be proportional to how much you put yourself out there, stretch beyond what you think you are capable of, and are willing to figure things out as you go.

Thought leadership is something you have to show up for – it's something you do, and then keep doing – so getting started is important, but it's only part of the picture. You also have to keep going. It's not a one-and-done activity. One white paper, one video, or one webinar isn't enough. Results accrue through repetition and consistency. You need to be able to sustain what you're doing over the long-term, which is why authenticity and alignment are so important, as well as the fire that keeps you going. You also need to balance comfort and challenge. If what you are doing feels too hard, you won't stick at it, but if it's not challenging you at all, you'll plateau.

A helpful framework for approaching this practically is the "Comfortable Corners of Thought Leadership" model (on the next page over) by our friend Bill Sherman of Thought Leadership Leverage in the United States. Bill has seen what I have both noticed and experienced; we seem to gravitate towards the few formats we're most comfortable with. Some, like Stan who we met in Chapter 6, prefer short-form. Stan's great at punchy posts and short videos, and he has to work hard to adapt his style and elaborate on his thinking as he writes his book.

Others, like me, prefer long-form content, editorial style articles where I get to explore ideas, or a book that allows me to make my case across a considerable word-count. Having a more natural mode is good, since this is where we will get the best expression of our thinking or ideas. However, Bill distinguishes between your level of comfort with the platform or modality and the degree of comfort you have with your ideas. This is the interplay we can start playing with as we balance comfort and challenge.

The Comfortable Corners of Thought Leadership

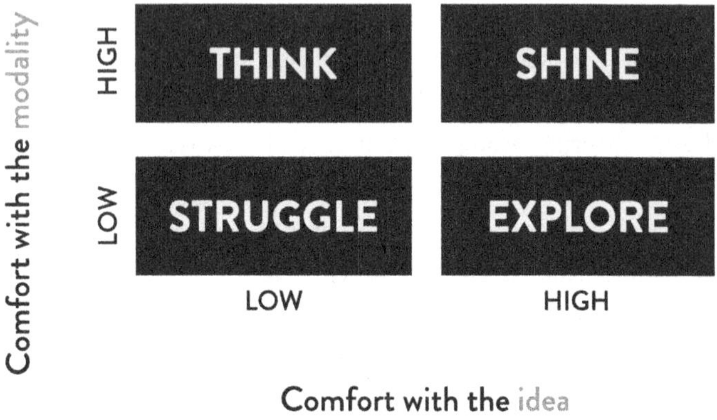

When you are still experimenting and exploring your ideas, start by utilising the formats that you are most comfortable with. If you are still playing with an idea, or have a concept that's not yet fully formed, a format that's natural for you allows you to *think* your way through it. We tend to do this naturally and instinctively already. I do this through writing, slowly iterating my ideas on the page to make them stronger. My husband, Logan, reaches for poster paper to draw or map it out visually. You might want to unpack and talk through a new idea as part of a podcast conversation.

Starting where you are most comfortable – and building confidence in what you're saying there first – will eventually allow you to *shine*. Then, as you explore the activities you're less comfortable with – showing up on video or speaking on stage, in my case – stick to the ideas that you feel well-versed in. This is why Verity and Nate suggested I be the one on the videos centred around books for thought leadership; this is my passion area so I was more willing to *explore* a new format when I could rely on the fact that I knew what I was talking about. The same will be true for you. Equally true, if you pick a modality that you don't have a lot of comfort with, and you're sharing ideas that you're still trying to weave stories or examples for, then you're likely to *struggle.*

Even before I came across Bill's framework, I was instinctively doing this – and there's every chance that you might be, too. We're adaptive and intuitive creatures who are great at finding ways to increase our comfort as we push (or are pushed) beyond the outer edges of our comfort zones. It's no secret that I don't enjoy presenting; I'm filled with a cold sense of dread when I have to get on stage and speak. The idea of delivering a keynote speech still remains terrifying to me. However, knowing that I need to be up there to gain visibility and credibility, and to share my perspective and ideas, I found a workaround. It was an alternative approach that helped me feel that I was lowering the stakes. Instead of delivering the main keynote address, I would opt for sitting on the panel, which somehow felt more manageable.

When I think about it in hindsight, this choice is amusing; I like to prepare and there is no way to do so in a live and impromptu panel discussion. I never know the questions ahead of time and am forced to think on my feet in the moment. This should be much more terrifying, surely? I think I was drawn to the format of a live question-and-answer panel because it aligns more with how I naturally show up. I don't need to be slick, polished and performative there, like I feel that I do to deliver a keynote. On a panel I am allowed to pause and think before I answer – or even think out loud as I am talking. This feels like a space that I can show up how I really am, while still getting to have visibility as one of the experts involved in events. It has seen me get on stage with less pressure – and who knows, maybe my comfort will increase until I can do it with more ease?

As we stretch and grow, our comfort zones also expand, so keep checking in with where you're at and what will keep you levelling up. We do this with our clients – either one-on-one, or in our small group coaching sessions – and there is value in surrounding yourself with people who are on a similar journey and will keep you moving forward.

Sometimes, though, you might notice for yourself and be able to shift the goalposts. This has been the case for me with video. For someone so shy about how she came across on camera, continuing to work during the Covid pandemic could have been a challenge. Yet somehow the huge surge in video calling that we needed to do during that time didn't bother me. When I was engaged in conversation with someone, all my self-consciousness fell away. We were using the medium that I'd once been so fearful of, but this was a totally different response. I didn't even seem to mind watching myself back on video afterwards; we would often record meetings and dip back into the footage when we didn't capture a key point well enough in our notes. This was another revelation for me. When I was in conversation, I didn't feel the same pressure or fear. I started to share videos that were snippets of meetings, conversations or interviews with people. And as I did so, I got more and more used to seeing myself on video.

Sensing my increased comfort with the format, I've since challenged myself to film more direct-to-camera clips to share on social media. Slowly but surely, I'm growing my skills and confidence in what I am able to do. It's also helped that I have been developing my ideas so intensely in writing this book; I've experienced greater comfort with my thinking. This is another way that building thought leadership becomes a virtuous cycle. Now I'm taking an activity that I abhorred and avoided, and doing it willingly and consistently.

4. Keep going

After you have started, you need to keep going. You need to do things on a regular basis. Real change takes time. One action or activity can create a spark, but sparks don't go anywhere without the long-haul gathering of tinder.[148] Momentum matters.

We know from the section on resistance (and Resistance) that it's more challenging to get something moving from a stand-still than it is to keep it moving when it is already in motion. So it is with ourselves. The ease I felt in being able to progress this book was directly correlated with how long it had been since I last looked at it. Similarly, after many months spent in lockdown, there were things I found challenging to do again. Getting three small children organised and out of the house on time, coordinating activities and social calendars. I was out of practice, so it took me a while, and more effort than previously, to get back into the swing of things after not doing them for so long. This is why it's so important to keep moving. To keep putting one foot in front of the other. It seems simple in theory, but proves much harder to do in practice. We're masters at inventing reasons – some of them highly plausible – not to do the thing.

Discipline matters much more than inspiration

I often have to remind people – including myself, but especially the other authors who I coach through writing their books – that discipline is important, even if it's not sexy. Many of us have romantic ideas that we will surf the waves of inspiration to a finished manuscript, or that we will always show up with the same fire, energy and excitement to bring to our work, but that is rarely the case. Our energy, moods, creativity and inspiration will ebb and flow. One of the chief mistakes I see people make – and still struggle with constantly myself – is thinking that they need to feel like doing the work in order to do the work.

The clincher for success is to show up anyway, regardless of how you are feeling. It's true that you might not feel like you can film a video on any given day. Nor can you necessarily always pull out the words you need, strung together just so, to furnish your next great written work. However, you can still show up in service of your thinking and ideas, and nudge your thought leadership activities forward in some way, with the following:

- use your block of thought leadership time to research and create opportunities to appear on podcasts
- develop a resource for your audience
- create a valuable piece of IP, or
- workshop a new model or framework with your team or a client.

You're still doing something to move your thinking forward in the time that you were planning to dedicate to thought leadership. Stay disciplined when it comes to doing something that increases your impact. Aim for a little bit more, or a little bit better, each day.

Set up systems for sustainability

As well as acting in alignment with your natural style and balancing comfort and challenge, the other thing that helps you keep going are systems. Again, setting up systems is certainly not sexy work, but the right sort of systems can be game-changing at keeping you on track and sustaining your activity.

Recall that one of the things we've noted already about successful thought leaders is that they are prolific. A large part of that comes from the fact that they are utilising some form of content system. Not only does a content system help you to keep communicating your thinking and ideas consistently – meaning you have to put some proactive work into developing and better articulating your ideas regularly – but it also cuts down on the work and creating that you ultimately need to do.

A good content system helps you to repurpose the content that you create. Say you deliver a webinar, present to a client or partner, or engage in a podcast-style conversation. This content alone can be broken into several short video or audio clips to share at different times, and with different blurbs, on social media. You could also write a blog about your conversation or topic and highlight key lessons. That blog can then be shared via social media in full, have various stories within it shared as shorter posts, have pull-quotes designed up to share with additional blurbs and be adapted into a slide carousel or an infographic for greater visual appeal and connection.

Content Breakdown Process

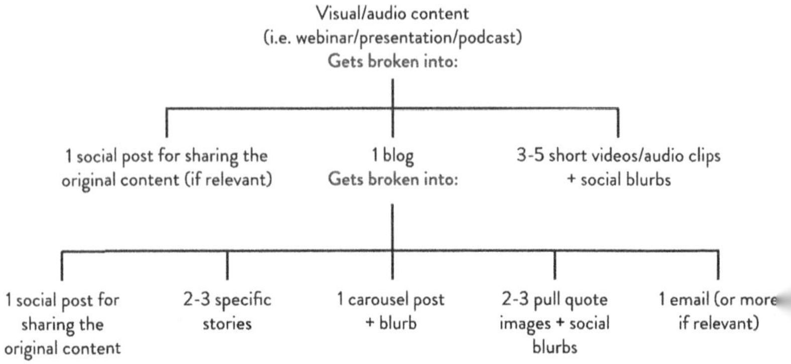

All this requires much less additional effort than thinking about and creating each individual piece of Acontent from scratch. It also allows you to forward-fill gaps in your content calendar. The specifics of your content system will be unique to you and your work, but think about where the opportunities lie in what you're already doing – and then consider any activities that you think would be fun to add.

It's incredibly common to worry about the content generation and communications aspect of thought leadership, but as you continue, and build the right habits, you'll find more than enough ideas for stories and content. You will be testing and trialling your thinking constantly, having conversations with people about what you do and encountering and solving problems. All of these provide opportunities if you keep your eyes and mind open for them.

If you're finding that you don't have enough opportunities or ideas, consider banding together with others who are on a similar path. Our clients in our Strategic Thought Leader programme love fleshing out their thinking together and getting additional ideas from each other (and our coaches) in their weekly calls; the accountability also helps to keep them focused and on-task, too.

However, you don't need to have something formal in place to create a system of accountability. Get friends or colleagues in your industry or similar together and form your own knowledge-sharing mastermind group. You can also look for opportunities with others who might already be hosting something like this. As our previously mentioned thought leadership programme and our Better Book Project continue to prove, support to stay on track is an important aspect of your sustainability systems.

There are so many ways around the things we think are barriers. Transcription software can help you get your ideas down without having to sit at a desk. Tools like Canva exist to help non-designers create great visual assets. You can enlist admin support, outsource aspects that you find tricky (often for a lower cost than you think), or partner with people who provide specialist services like writing support or ideation sessions to enhance your ideas. Your systems should be based on what you need and what will work best for you, but surrounding yourself with others who are on a similar journey to you, and will continue to push you further, is incredibly valuable.

Communicating your ideas consistently is going to become a business-as-usual aspect of what you're doing to increase your impact, creating a virtuous cycle of momentum and impact. However, for some, once it becomes "just another thing that you do", it can also become a bit boring. It's also only one part – albeit an important part – of what you'll be doing. The other part of setting up systems is concerned with how you will keep levelling up and moving ever closer to the impact that you want.

When we coach clients, regular check-ins and reviews allow us to reflect and provide a friendly push. You can certainly set up mini check-ins with yourself (e.g. each month or each quarter) where you similarly look at what's working, what isn't, and what's next. Another strategy, and an aspect of our programme that has worked well, is that we focus our activity around both the business-as-usual stuff and regular sprints.

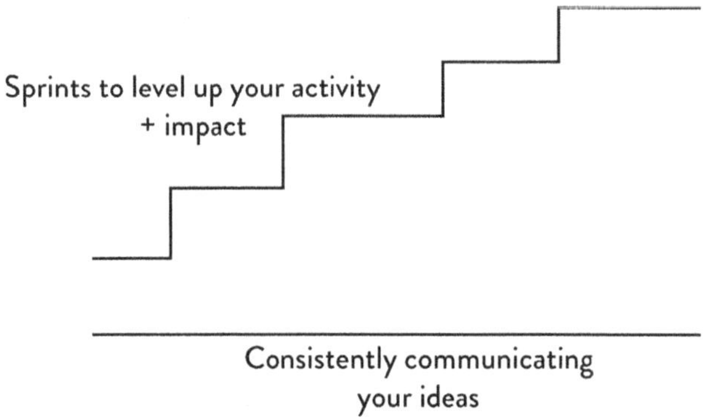

Increasing your impact is like building a brick wall. You do this incrementally, all the while connecting new additions securely to what's already there so that your wall remains stable. You'll start with a low wall, which is sturdy because you are consistently communicating your ideas to build trust and increase your audience over time. From there, your sprints or focused projects enable you to make your wall higher. They are what push you further and ensure you maintain momentum, motivation and excitement about the impact that you're creating.

A final piece of advice: constructive comparisons only

The other last thing I want you to do as you stay the course in building thought leadership and contributing to the collective ideascape is keep focused on your own race. As you do this work, you are inevitably going to come across and engage with more people who are sharing their thinking out in the world, too. And just like how you take much more notice of the colour of people's bathrooms when you're narrowing down paint swatches for your bathroom revamp, or you start seeing blue cars everywhere on the road when you decide you're in the market for one, you will likely become more aware of the activity that others are doing to put their thinking out into the world with impact when you're proactively doing the same. This can be a good thing, as it can provide clues and ideas around what you could be doing (in your own, unique way, of course), but it can similarly be dangerous territory. The key is to look at what others are doing for inspiration, not with judgements. Again, comparison is the thief of joy.

In a TED podcast, Adam Grant was interviewed about his latest book, *Hidden Potential.* Grant was sharing his story about when he wanted to do more public speaking. He threw himself in the deep end, and started before he was ready, as we have seen. But Grant went on to explain that, when he wanted to level up his speaking, he turned to learning from other great speakers. The first thing he did was watch a video of Martin Luther King's 'I Have a Dream' speech. 'It was completely demoralising,' Grant laughs. He was resigned to the fact he would never be as good King and his iconic speech, no matter how hard he worked.[149] He figured he might as well give up, because it seemed so impossible.

But Grant goes on to detail a common error that he was making – one that we've all likely made. Grant was assuming that what he was observing in Martin Luther King was innate. He wasn't considering the fact that King had grown up in an oral culture, that he had watched his father and others preach countless sermons, and that he himself was well-practiced. The year that King gave his 'I Have a Dream' speech, he had given over 350 speeches, not to mention the 20 years of deliberate practice in public speaking that he had under his belt by that point.

It's hard to see all the history when we're on the outside looking in. Rather, it seems impossible to imagine that Martin Luther King could have ever been a novice – a learning, experimenting speaker. Grant refers to this as our 'unfortunate access to greatness'. We see people at their peak and assume that they started far ahead of us.

Every single person who has achieved incredible impact has been on a journey to do so. They have started before they felt completely ready. They have taken their inner critics along for the ride. They have worried that they didn't have what it takes. They have had to challenge some norm, expectation or established way of doing things. But they have shown up time and time again in service of their ideas and the people that they are there for because they couldn't not. Because they were too uncomfortable with the status quo to leave it untouched. This is your call to do the same.

AFTERWORD

What if you turned your magic all the way up?

You already have everything you need to make the change you want to see.

I hope that is clear by this point. It wasn't always for me.

I started this book with, frankly, wishful thinking. I *wanted* my idea – that there was room for all the people who had great ideas and were doing great work to have incredible impact – to be true.

I wanted it to be true for a couple of reasons. The first was that the traditional notion of thought leadership is, as we've seen, a relatively narrow one, made for (and largely by) the sage on the stage archetype. Reading the room, you'd get the impression that a high-volume personality is a prerequisite for thought leadership success. There is some truth in that: we tend to listen to the loudest voices first. But how can a quiet type, like me, hope to compete if those are the rules of the game? I wouldn't even make it past the try-outs.

I remember sitting in class when I was younger. I rarely contributed to the discussion; that was too scary. But I was always watching, listening and processing. I would hear the answers ventured by those who were brave enough to speak up and I would think, *Well, perhaps, but that's only part of it!* I believed that what I had – what I held back – was a better answer, or a fuller, more complete view. I could see, even back then, that just because I wasn't saying it as loudly didn't mean that I didn't have something valuable to say.

The other reason that I want my idea to be right and true is that now that I've poked at this dominant idea of thought leadership for a while, and worked in the field for a number of years, I can see that it's not just the loud voices or charismatic personalities that we need.

Anyone with a unique perspective, valuable idea, and the desire to have a positive impact on the world can – and should – be a thought leader. Even if you don't always sound slick and polished, even if you don't want to take up lots of space, even if you don't want to act bold or brash in sharing what you're doing.

Thought leadership is for those who are prepared to make things authentically better.

Writing this book has been part of my own journey in claiming my voice. And it's been hard, which may come as a surprise to you. I am a full-time writer, running a thought leadership agency whose primary outputs are thinking (via coaching) and writing. While I give a piece of myself to every client I work with and output I produce, this book has asked a lot from me over the last year or so of thinking, stress-testing, writing, editing, writing more, editing more, countless reads and re-reads, and finally getting it into the form you have with you today.

This book has been hard because it's seen me challenged at every turn. Wanting an idea to be true doesn't make it so. Our ideas need to be stress-tested, backed into a corner, and have their strength proven. This process is hard work with a client, but a special kind of existential threat when it's your idea – your personality, strengths, and what you've shaped your identity on – being tested. It takes a different realness, and it brings up a fair bit of imposter syndrome, when you're also your own editor.

But the result of this challenging, circuitous route isn't just a stronger book, but a stronger Christina. There's a virtuous cycle that happens when we're devoting time to ideas development – to our thinking – and it wouldn't have happened if I hadn't: (a) taken the time to develop my thinking; and (b) been convinced that I could own my own, authentic, quiet thought leadership, while showing others that they can step into theirs also.

Discovering your own thought leadership, at whatever volume, and in whatever way, is a step towards recognising and utilising the power within you. It's a launching-off point, one that sees you able to shape the world around you to be one that's simply better, in whatever terms matter to you.

I've seen first-hand the benefit of working with diverse people and how it makes teams more creative, innovative, and inclusive. The best teams I've worked in have had a mixture of quiet and loud people working together. My closest relationships – with Verity at work and my husband Logan at home – also seem to be with people who have that dominant natural style. It makes sense that we tend to be drawn to people with the traits or qualities that we admire, but don't feel that we possess ourselves. But not only have I come to love, admire and respect these two, but, in my relationships with them, I have also gained a deeper appreciation for my own style and strengths.

We are all works-in-progress. The journey to becoming a thought leader is ongoing, and the path will be as unique as you are.

Recognising that there's room for everyone to find their voice and be heard, and that alternative paths are both valid and valuable, allows us all to benefit. Imagine what your workplace or home or community could look like if everyone had a chance to pursue their own authentic perspective with confidence, and share that in the discussions that count. Beyond that, imagine if we all got to see that what we do and think matters, that it has an impact, and that each of us can make – and are making – a difference.

Because here's where it comes full circle for me. There's an additional reason that I want everyone who has great ideas, and who wants to own their own voice, to be able to have the impact they want. And that reason is my kids.

Kids teach us a lot. I know that's a cliché, but it's true. I've learned so much as a parent, and not just about parenting. I have three little boys – all under the age of 10 – who are such different little humans; variously vocal, introspective, adventurous, logical and (let's be honest) challenging. But all of them are curious, creative and brave. It's an absolute joy to see them not only explore, but increase their understanding of, our world.

Every night at our dinner table, Logan asks everyone to share the most fun thing they did that day – or sometimes it's something we are proud of, or perhaps something we found tricky. Amid getting up from the table countless times to find and fill drink bottles, the boys will rattle off their various answers in turn. And still with his consultant hat on, even when he gets home, Logan will invariably prompt them with further questions: 'What made that fun?' and 'What did you learn doing that?' These conversations provide a precious window into how they engage with the things and the people around them. They are completely different little people and yet they all have their own totally valid ways of showing up, solving problems, and explaining the world around them.

I look at the three of them, with so much ahead of them and all currently so comfortable with their own ways of looking at the world, and it deepens the hope I have. I want them to always know that they have everything they need to be successful on their own terms. It's up to us to help them and others find a place, on their own terms – as we each find our own places, too.

We believe in better

At Intelligent Ink, we help experts in their fields drive meaningful change with their ideas.

Visit **www.intelligentink.co.nz/better** for free resources and tools to help you on your journey towards bigger impact.

You can also follow Christina Wedgwood on LinkedIn to access her newsletter.

INTELLIGENT INK
CLEVER THINGS WITH WORDS

Thank you

I published my first book when I was just eight years old (entitled *The Magic Pencil*) and for years writing books has been a large part of what I do for clients. I'd either written, contributed to, or edited more than 18 books before I sat down to write this one. I thought I knew all that was involved and would be able to write a book relatively easily. This book proved me wrong.

It turns out it's a lot harder to wrangle your own ideas than it is to structure and articulate other people's.

For this reason, writing this book was absolutely a team effort, and I could not have done it without my team of incredible Inkers. Thank you all for your steadfast support throughout this process – for taking on more of the client load, for never questioning if this was what I should be spending my time on, and for just generally and generously standing behind me the whole way.

Verity: You have always valued and appreciated our differences and helped me to amplify my strengths.

Dave: You knew what I was trying to do and say here (even when I didn't), and you applied the perfect amount of pressure and push – coaching me to my own answers artfully, instead of inserting your own.

Elsa: You picked it up at the most crucial part of the project and carried both the book and me across the finish-line. For that I'm immensely grateful.

Beyond this team, I want to thank all of my clever clients and the passionate people in my professional network. So many of you inspire me daily, and you've all contributed to this book through your insights, reflections and advice. I am so lucky to be surrounded by such smart and generous people, and I truly learn more from all of you than I could ever hope to teach.

Thank you to all of my friends and family who took an interest in what I was doing, asked questions and worked to stop your eyes from glazing over when I went into full rants. I could feel you cheering me on, even when you didn't really know what I was going on about! I appreciate your practical support, love and encouragement.

Thank you to my boys for being among my greatest teachers. You are all so different, and yet you all have so much to offer the world. I love that you are so excited for me having done this, that you've never once begrudged how much time I have lost at my desk, and that you're so keen to have your 'own copy to keep' now that the book is done.

And a final thank you goes to my husband, Logan. You've provided so much practical support in order for me to do this – but, far more than that, you've maintained your unwavering belief in me and in my ideas. You push me to do better, pull me out of my spirals, and, because you never doubt me, I keep finding my way forward. I love you.

Bibliography

Agarwal, Amit. "Why Are TED Talks 18 Minutes Long?" *Digital Inspiration,* February 15, 2010, https://www.labnol.org/tech/ted-talk-18-minutes/12755/.

Ali, Mustahsan. "What Is Consultative Leadership?" LinkedIn, January 4, 2022, https://www.linkedin.com/pulse/what-consultative-leadership-mustahsan-ali/.

Anderson, Michael and Elias Mossialos. "Beyond Gross Domestic Product for New Zealand's Wellbeing Budget." *The Lancet Public Health* 4, no 7 (2019): 320–21, https://doi.org/10.1016/S2468-2667(19)30109-4.

Attar, Samar. *Debunking the Myths of Colonization: The Arabs and Europe.* Lanham: University Press of America, 2010.

Beck, James W., Alison E. Carr, and Philip T. Walmsley. "What Have You Done for Me Lately? Charisma Attenuates the Decline in U.S. Presidential Approval Over Time." *The Leadership Quarterly* 23, no. 5 (2012): 934–42, https://doi.org/10.1016/j.leaqua.2012.06.002.

Bell, Bex. *Inner Critic to Inner Coach: How to Heal the Imposter Syndrome, End Self-sabotage and Own Your Greatness.* Auckland: Upstart Press, 2024.

Berger, Jonah. *Magic Words: What to Say to Get Your Way.* New York: Harper Business, 2023.

Berkeley Executive Education. "The Importance of Authenticity." *Berkeley ExecEd Insights,* December 17, 2019, https://executive.berkeley.edu/thought-leadership/blog/importance-authenticity.

Blake, Craig. "How Oversimplifying a Complex World Drives Us Apart." *Medium,* July 31, 2018, https://craigblake.medium.com/how-oversimplifying-a-complex-world-drives-us-apart-caf26506ccdf

Bogart, Julie. *Raising Critical Thinkers: A Parent's Guide to Growing Wise Kids in the Digital Age.* New York: Penguin Putnam Inc., 2023.

Boyes, Alice. "5 Mistakes We Make When We're Overwhelmed." *Harvard Business Review,* April 27, 2021, https://hbr.org/2021/04/5-mistakes-we-make-when-were-overwhelmed.

Brosseau, Denise. *Ready to be a Thought Leader?: How to Increase Your Influence, Impact, and Success.* San Francisco: Jossey-Bass, 2014.

Burkeman, Oliver. *The Antidote: Happiness for People Who Can't Stand Positive Thinking.* New York: Macmillan Farrar, Straus and Giroux, 2013.

Cain, Susan. *Quiet: The Power of Introverts in a World That Can't Stop Talking.* New York: Crown Publishing Group, 2013.

Camuffo, Arnaldo, Alessandro Cordova, Alfonso Gambardella, and Chiara Spina. "A Scientific Approach to Entrepreneurial Decision Making: Evidence from a Randomised Control Trial." *Management Science 66* (2020): 564–86, doi/10.1287/mnsc.2018.3249.

Carlson, Nicholas. "Facebook: Cash-Flow Positive with 300 Million Users." *Business Insider,* September 16, 2009, https://www.businessinsider.com/facebook-cash-flow-positive-with-300-million-users-2009-9.

Carlyle, Thomas. *On Heroes, Hero-worship, and the Heroic in History: Six Lectures.* New York: D. Appleton and Company, 1841.

Carr, Nicholas. *The Shallows: What the Internet is Doing to Our Brains.* New York: WW Norton & Co, 2011.

Chaffee, Sarah, "Nature Agrees: Science Students Should 'Actively Grapple with Questions' Not Just 'Listen to Answers'." *Evolution News & Science Today,* August 5, 2015, https://evolutionnews.org/2015/08/nature_agrees_i/.

Chamorro-Premuzic, Tomas. *Why Do So Many Incompetent Men Become Leaders? (And How to Fix It).* Brighton, MA: Harvard Business Review Press, 2019.

Charmley, John. *Churchill: The End of Glory: A Political Biography.* New York: Harcourt Brace, 1993.

Chia, Sam. "6 Management Styles: Advantages and Disadvantages." *BetterUp*, November 8, 2021, https://www.betterup.com/blog/management-styles.

Church, Matt. *The Thought Leaders Practice.* Sydney: Thought Leaders, 2016.

Clear, James. *Atomic Habits: An Easy and Proven Way to Build Good Habits and Break Bad Ones.* New York: Avery, 2018.

Clear, James "Life Rewards Action LinkedIn, 2023, https://www.linkedin.com/posts/jamesclear_life-rewards-action-not-intelligence-many-activity-7080198464646623232-N8-j/.

Clear, James. "Successful People Start Before They Feel Ready." *James Clear Blog,* accessed April 2, 2023, https://jamesclear.com/successful-people-start-before-they-feel-ready.

Comstock, Beth. *Imagine It Forward: Courage, Creativity, and the Power of Change.* New York: Crown Currency, 2018.

Curran, Thomas. *The Perfection Trap: Embracing the Power of Good Enough.* New York: Scribner, 2023.

Davis, Pete. *Dedicated: The Case for Commitment in an Age of Infinite Browsing.* New York: Simon & Schuster, 2021.

Dean, Alexandra, director. *Bombshell: The Hedy Lamarr Story.*

Kino Lorber & Zeitgeist Films, November 24, 2017, Google Play.

De Bono, Edward. *Teach Your Child How to Think.* New York: Penguin Books, 1994.

DeGruttola, Megan. "Survey Reveals How Consumers Really Judge Brand Authenticity (and Influencers)." *Social Media Today,* February 25, 2019, https://www.socialmediatoday.com/news/survey-reveals-how-consumers-really-judge-brand-authenticity-and-influence/549038/.

Dobelli, Rolf. *The Art of Thinking Clearly.* New York: HarperCollins, 2014.

Duranti, Marco. *The Conservative Human Rights Revolution: European Identity, Transnational Politics, and the Origins of the European Convention.* Oxford: Oxford University Press, 2016.

Edmondson, Amy. *Right Kind of Wrong: The Science of Failing Well.* New York: Simon & Schuster Atria, 2023.

Ehret, Michael G. "Common Leadership Strategies and Practices Among Authentic Senior Leaders" *Pepperdine Digital Common Theses and Dissertations* 708 (2016), https://digitalcommons.pepperdine.edu/etd/708.

Elkins, Kathleen. "Richard Branson Wears 'the Same Pair of Jeans Every Day'—Here's How It Could Contribute to His Success." *CNBC,* June 7, 2019, https://www.cnbc.com/2019/06/07/why-successful-people-wear-the-same-thing-every-day.html.

Endedijk, H.M., M. Meyer, H. Bekkering, A.H.N. Cillessen, and S. Hunnius. "Neural Mirroring and Social Interaction: Motor System Involvement During Action Observation Relates to Early Peer Cooperation." *Developmental Cognitive Neuroscience* 24, (2017): 33–41, https://doi.org/10.1016/j.dcn.2017.01.001.

Firestein, Stuart. *Ignorance: How it Drives Science.* New York: Oxford University Press, 2012.

Firestone, Randall S. "Oversimplification in Philosophy." *Open Journal of Philosophy* 9, (2019): 396–427, doi: 10.4236/ojpp.2019.93025.

Ford, Ellen Joan. "Award Winning Leader, Military Veteran, International Speaker and Facilitator." Accessed March 27, 2024, https://www.ellenjoanford.com/about.

Freund, Phillip Alexander and Nadine Kasten. "How Smart Do You Think You Are? A Meta-analysis on the Validity of Self-estimates of Cognitive Ability." *Psychological Bulletin* 138, no. 2 (2012): 296–321, https://doi.org/10.1037/a0026556.

Galef, Julia. *The Scout Mindset: Why Some People See Things Clearly and Others Don't.* New York: Penguin Portfolio, 2021.

Gaston, Meredith. *Find Your Sparkle: Embracing the Magic of Life.* Hardie Grant Books, 2019.

Gilbert, Ben. "Sheryl Sandberg Joined Facebook When it was a Startup, Just Months Before the 2008 Recession. Here's How She Says Facebook Strengthened Its Business During the Downturn, and Her Advice to Startups That are Struggling Now." *Business Insider,* April 2, 2020, https://www.businessinsider.com/sheryl-sandberg-on-how-facebook-survived-the-2008-financial-crash-2020-4.

Godin, Seth. *Song of Significance: A New Manifesto for Teams.* New York: Penguin Portfolio, 2023.

Grant, Adam, *Hidden Potential: The Science of Achieving Greater Things*. New York: Viking, 2023.

Grant, Adam. "How I Overcame the Fear of Public Speaking." *University of Michigan Center for Positive Organizations Press,* September 18, 2014, https://positiveorgs.bus.umich.edu/news/how-i-overcame-the-fear-of-public-speaking/.

Grant, Adam. *Originals: How Non-Conformists Change the World.* New York: WH Allen, 2017.

Grant, Adam. *Think Again: The Power of Knowing What You Don't Know.* New York: Viking, 2021.

Grant, Adam and Malcolm Gladwell. "Unlocking Hidden Potential with Malcolm Gladwell." *TED,* podcast, October 24, 2023, https://www.ted.com/podcasts/worklife/unlocking-hidden-potential-with-malcolm-gladwell-transcript?utm_source=substack&utm_medium=email.

Grant, Adam M., Francesca Gino, and David A. Hofmann. "Reversing the Extraverted Leadership Advantage: The Role of Employee Proactivity." *Academy of Management Journal* 54, no. 3 (2011), https://doi.org/10.5465/amj.2011.61968043.

Haden, Jeff. "Science Says Stop Infecting Other People with the 'Better Than Average' Effect." *Inc. Australia*, February 14, 2020, https://www.inc-aus.com/jeff-haden/science-says-stop-infecting-other-people-with-better-than-average-effect.html.

Hagmann, David and George Loewenstein. "Persuasion with Motivated Beliefs." Opinion Dynamics and Collective Decisions Working Paper. Pittsburgh, PA: Carnegie Mellon University, 2017, 1–29, https://nf.vse.cz/wp-content/uploads/page/995/Hagmann.pdf.

Hari, Johann. *Stolen Focus: Why You Can't Pay Attention – And How to Think Deeply Again.* New York: Crown Publishing Group, 2022.

Hersey, Paul, Kenneth H. Blanchard, and Dewey E. Johnson. *Management of Organizational Behavior: Utilizing Human Resources.* Philadelphia: Pennsylvania State University Press, 1996.

Hewitt, D.G. "Double Oh Fail: 10 of the Most Inept Spies in the History of Espionage." *History Collection,* May 10, 2018, https://historycollection.com/double-oh-fail-10-of-the-most-inept-spies-in-the-history-of-espionage/#heinrich-albert.

Hines, Marion, John Murray, and Moira Lawler. "Better Together. Lifewise Annual Report 2015." *Lifewise,* https://www.lifewise.org.nz/wp-content/uploads/2016/03/2015-annual-report.pdf.

Hoedel, Joe. "Jerry Rice – Discipline." *Character Development and Leadership,* accessed May 15, 2024, https://characterandleadership.com/jerry-rice-discipline/.

Hoeks, John, Lauri A. Stowe, Petra Hendriks, and Harm Brouwer. "Questions Left Unanswered: How the Brain Responds to Missing Information." *PLoS ONE* 8, no. 10 (2013): e73594, https://doi.org/10.1371/journal.pone.0073594

Hoekstra, Rutger. *This is the Moment to Go Beyond GDP*. WWF, Wellbeing Economy Alliance, and European Environmental Bureau, 2022, https://weall.org/wp-content/uploads/This-is-the-moment-to-go-Beyond-GDP-web-1.pdf

Holmes, Jamie. "The Case for Teaching Ignorance." *New York Times,* August 24, 2015, https://www.nytimes.com/2015/08/24/opinion/the-case-for-teaching-ignorance.html.

Huffington, Arianna. *Thrive: The Third Metric to Redefining Success and Creating a Life of Well-Being, Wisdom, and Wonder*. New York: Harmony Books, 2014.

Jeong, Martha, Leslie K. John, Francesca Gino, and Laura Huang. "Research: Changing Your Mind Makes You Seem Intelligent." *Harvard Business Review,* September 11, 2019, https://hbr.org/2019/09/research-changing-your-mind-makes-you-seem-intelligent.

John, Leslie K., Martha Jeong, Francesca Gino, and Laura Huang. "The Self-Presentational Consequences of Upholding One's Stance in Spite of the Evidence." *Organizational Behavior and Human Decision Processes* 154, (2019): 1–14. https://doi.org/10.1016/j.obhdp.2019.07.001.

Jones, Don. "A Guide to the Sidelines: Four Key Conversations for Coaches." *Edutopia*, March 22, 2015, https://www.edutopia.org/discussion/guide-sidelines.

Karmarkar, Uma R. and Zakary L. Tormala. "Believe Me, I Have No Idea What I'm Talking About: The Effects of Source Certainty on Consumer Involvement and Persuasion." *Journal of Consumer Research* 36, no. 6. (2010): 1033–49, https://doi.org/10.1086/648381.

Kashdan, Todd B. *The Art of Insubordination: How to Dissent and Defy Effectively.* New York: Avery, 2022.

Kelley, David. "How to Build Your Creative Confidence." TED. May 16, 2012. YouTube video, https://www.youtube.com/watch?v=16p9YRF0l-g.

Kempton, Beth. *The Way of the Fearless Writer: Mindful Wisdom For a Flourishing Writing Life.* New York: Macmillan St Martin's Essentials, 2023.

Kleon, Austin. *Steal Like and Artist: 10 Things Nobody Told You About Being Creative.* New York: Hachette Workman Press, 2012.

Kruger, Justin and David Dunning. "Unskilled and Unaware of It: How Difficulties in Recognising One's Own Incompetence Lead to Inflated Self-Assessments." *Journal of Personality and Social Psychology* 77, no. 6 (1999): 1121–34, https://doi.org/10.2139/ssrn.1114332.

Langworth, Richard M. "Churchill, Women's Suffrage, and 'Black Friday,' November 1910." *The Churchill Project Hillsdale College,* August 7, 2018, https://winstonchurchill.hillsdale.edu/churchill-womens-suffrage-black-friday/.

Lipman, Matthew. "About P4C." *P4CNZ Philosophy for Children New Zealand,* accessed May 15, 2020, https://www.p4c.org.nz/about/.

Main, Paul. "Assimilation vs Accommodation." *Structural Learning,* April 28, 2023, https://www.structural-learning.com/post/assimilation-vs-accommodation.

Marcus, Bob. "Evolving Leadership from Command and Control to Empowerment and Collaboration." LinkedIn, February 18, 2020, https://www.linkedin.com/pulse/evolving-leadership-from-command-and-control-bob-marcus/.

McAlpine, Suzi. *Beyond Burnout: How to Spot It, Stop It and Stamp it Out.* Auckland: Penguin Books, 2021.

McAlpine, Suzi. "Make Like a Chameleon – Why Situational Leadership is Key in 2024." *The Leader's Digest,* January 23, 2024, https://suzimcalpine.com/make-like-a-chameleon-why-situational-leadership-is-key-in-2024/.

McKeown, Greg. *Effortless: Make It Easier to Do What Matters Most.* London: Ebury Edge, 2021.

McKeown, Greg. *Essentialism: The Disciplined Pursuit of Less.* New York: Crown Currency, 2014.

McKeown, Greg (host). "The Quiet Person with the Answer." *The Greg McKeown Podcast, https://gregmckeown.com/podcast/episode/the-quiet-person-with-the-answer/.*

Mercier, Hugo and Dan Sperber. *The Enigma of Reason.* Cambridge, MA: Harvard University Press, 2017.

Mohr, Tara. *Playing Big: Practical Wisdom for Women Who Want to Speak Up, Create, and Lead.* New York: Avery, 2015.

Myers, Chris. "Why Oversimplification is Bad for Entrepreneurs, Consumers, and Society As a Whole." *Forbes*, August 5, 2016, https://www.forbes.com/sites/chrismyers/2016/08/05/why-oversimplification-is-bad-for-entrepreneurs-consumers-and-society-as-a-whole/.

Paul, Annie Murphy. *The Extended Mind: The Power of Thinking Outside the Brain.* Boston: Mariner Books, 2021.

Peppin, Aidan. "Pieces in the Puzzle: Why We Need to Convene Diverse Voices." *Ada Lovelace Institute.* October29, 2019, https://www.adalovelaceinstitute.org/blog/why-we-need-to-convene-diverse-voices/.

Phenomena. "The Pulse of the Times: Exploring the Concept of Zeitgeist." *Phenomena.org.* n.d., https://www.phenomena.org/the-pulse-of-the-times-exploring-the-concept-of-zeitgeist/.

Phillips, Katherine W. "How Diversity Makes Us Smarter". *Scientific American.* October 2014, https://www.scientificamerican.com/article/how-diversity-makes-us-smarter/.

Piaget, John. *The Construction of Reality in the Child* [*La Construction du Réel chez l'Enfant*, 1935]. New York: Basic Books, 1954.

Pilling, David. *The Growth Delusion: Wealth, Poverty, and the Well-being of Nations.* New York: Crown Publishing Group, 2019.

Pollard, Matthew. *The Introvert's Edge: How the Quiet and Shy Can Outsell Anyone.* New York: HarperCollins, 2018.

Pratt, Mary. K. and Francesca Sales. "What is Authentic Leadership?" *TechTarget*, August 2023, https://www.techtarget.com/searchcio/definition/authentic-leadership.

Pressfield, Steven. *The War of Art: Break Through the Blocks and Win Your Inner Creative Battles.* New York: Black Irish Entertainment, 2012.

QI. "Hoaxes starring Danny Baker, Sean Lock, and David Mitchell." (Series H, episode 3). Produced by BBC. Aired October 1, 2010 on BBC One.

Ripley, Amanda, *High Conflict: Why We Get Trapped and How We Get Out.* New York: Simon & Schuster, 2021.

Russell, Bertrand. "The Triumph of Stupidity." *New York American,* May 10, 1933, 203–204.

Santos-Pinto, Luis. "Labor Market Signaling and Self-Confidence: Wage Compression and the Gender Pay Gap." *Journal of Labor Economics* 30, no. 4 (2012): 873–914, https://doi.org/10.1086/666646.

Saul, Isaac. "People Ask Me All the Time …" [Post]. X, October 11, 2023, https://twitter.com/Ike_Saul/status/1711780282725011520.

Servar, Margarita. "How Long Should a LinkedIn Post or Message Be?" *Linkedin Helper Blog,* June 16, 2023, https://www.linkedhelper.com/blog/linkedin-character-limit/.

Sietz, Kerry. "Please Unmute Me: The Importance of Listening to Diverse Voices." *Simmons University Institute for Inclusive Leadership,* May 21, 2021, https://www.inclusiveleadership.com/research-insights/please-unmute-me-the-importance-of-listening-to-diverse-voices/.

Sincero, Jen. *You are a Badass: How to Stop Doubting Your Greatness and Start Living an Awesome Life.* Philadelphia: Running Press, 2013.

SpeakersU. "Best Business Speakers of 2023: A Comprehensive Guide to the Best in the Industry." *SpeakersU Guides,* accessed April 2, 2023, https://speakersu.com/guides/best-business-speakers-of-2023/.

Stanier, Michael Bungay. 'Can You Turn on Authentic?' [Email]. August 24, 2023.

Stanier, Michael Bungay. *How to Work with (Almost) Anyone: Five Questions for Building the Best Possible Relationships.* Vancouver: Page Two, 2023.

Tucker, Robert B. "How Crowdsourcing Can Enhance Innovation Performance." *Forbes,* June 16, 2017, https://www.forbes.com/sites/robertbtucker/2017/06/16/how-crowdsourcing-can-enhance-innovation-performance/.

van der Bles, Anne Marthe, Sander van der Linden, Alexandra L.J. Freeman, and David J. Spiegelhalter. "The Effects of Communicating Uncertainty on Public Trust in Facts and Numbers." *Proceedings of the National Academy of Sciences* 117, no. 14 (2020): 7672–83, https://doi.org/10.1073/pnas.1913678117.

Wickham, Robert E. "Perceived Authenticity in Romantic Partners." *Journal of Experimental Social Psychology* 49, no. 5(2013): 878–87, https://doi.org/10.1016/j.jesp.2013.04.001.

Wood, Alex M., Alex P. Linley, John Maltby, Michael Baliousis, and Stephen Joseph. "The Authentic Personality: A Theoretical and Empirical Conceptualization and the Development of the Authenticity Scale." *Journal of Counseling Psychology* 55, no. 3 (2008): 385–99, https://doi.org/10.1037/0022-0167.55.3.385.

Zucker, Rebecca and Darin Rowell. "6 Strategies for Leading Through Uncertainty." *Harvard Business Review,* April 26, 2021, https://hbr.org/2021/04/6-strategies-for-leading-through-uncertainty

Endnotes

1 There are increasingly more places for change to emerge: Comstock, *Imagine it Forward*.

2 Argument leads to more innovative solutions: Paul, *The Extended Mind*.

3 Mahatma Gandhi quote: found in Ripley, *High Conflict*, 242.

4 Talkers are perceived as smarter than quieter people: Cain, *Quiet*, p.51

5 'We get stuck following people who dominate the discussion': Grant, *Hidden Potential*, p.183.

6 Intelligence doesn't correlate with the amount people talk: Cain, *Quiet*, p.51

7 There is little difference between quiet and louder people: ibid.

8 Charisma tends to cover for bad performance in presidents: Beck et al., "What Have You Done for Me Lately?" p.2.

9 Respect is based on verbal abilities, not originality: Cain, *Quiet*, p.77.

10 Ibid., p.3.

11 Bad ideas prevail: Cain, Quiet, p.51.

12 Ibid., p.164.

13 Ibid.

14 Facebook has over 3 billion users: Gilbert, "Sheryl Sandberg Joined Facebook."

15 Facebook went back to the basics to adapt: Gilbert, "Sheryl Sandberg Joined Facebook."

16 Facebook reported being cashflow-positive in 2009: Carlson, "Facebook: Cash-Flow Positive."

17 'Our reverence for alpha status blinds us': Cain, *Quiet*, p.12.

18 Diversity creates a more accurate view: Peppin, "Pieces in the Puzzle."

19 Groups of similar racial identity assumed they all held the same information and perspective: Phillips, "How Diversity Makes Us Smarter."

20 Diversity of voices results in greater innovation and higher productivity: Sietz, "Please Unmute Me."

21 'It's the quiet ones that hold the answers': McKeown, podcast.

22 Chemistry class was Hedwig's favourite: *Bombshell*, directed by Alexandra Dean.

23 Characterisations of the Zeitgeist: Phenomena, "The Pulse of the Times."

24 The brain as a magpie: Paul, *The Extended Mind*, p.11

25 Ibid., p.215

26 Examples of thinkers who thrived in isolation: Cain, *Quiet*, p.78.

27 Authentic leadership models encourage sincere and genuine management styles: Pratt and Sales, "What is Authentic Leadership?"

28 There is a gap in the traits and behaviours between effective leadership and being chosen to lead: Chamorro-Premuzic, *Why Do So Many Incompetent Men Become Leaders?*

29 We tend to assume we are better than we are: Santos-Pinto, "Labor Market Signaling", p.873.

30 10 percent overlap between smarts and perceptions: Freund and Kasten, "How Smart Do You Think You Are?" p.296.

31 80 percent of people think they are above-average drivers: Haden, "Science Says Stop Infecting Other People ..."

32 Experts and clueless people don't differ much in their self-perception: Kruger and Dunning, "Unskilled and Unaware ...", p.1121.

33 'The fundamental cause of the trouble is that in the modern world the stupid are cocksure while the intelligent are full of doubt': Russell, "The Triumph of Stupidity", pp.203–204.

34 Lifewise end-of-year statistics: Hines et al., "Better Together. Lifewise Annual Report 2015."

35 Ellen Joan Ford has significantly influenced how the army is now approaching diversity challenges, testimonial on: Ford, "Award Winning Leader ..."

36 Story of Jerry Rice: Hoedel, "Jerry Rice – Discipline."

37 Story of Heinrich Albert: Hewitt, "Double Oh Fail."

38 'Women think traditional expertise is the only kind of legitimate qualification': Mohr, Playing Big, p.212.

39 Ibid., p.214.

40 Real knowledge is differentiated from "chauffeur knowledge": Dobelli, *The Art of Thinking Clearly.*

41 'We naturally default to finding all the ways we're "not good enough"': Bell, *Inner Critic to Inner Coach,* p.50.

42 "We've just woken the sleeping guard at the edge of our comfort zone": Mohr, *Playing Big*, p.110.

43 The concept of 'the anxious roommate' in your head: Huffington, *Thrive.*

44 People 'grapple with self-doubt because they are playing it big': Mohr, *Playing Big,* p.15.

45 'Defeating resistance is like giving birth': Pressfield, *The War of Art,* p.57.

46 Courage isn't the absence of fear, but a 'willingness to do things that are so important': Godin, *Song of Significance,* p.74.

47 Authenticity dates back to ancient Greek philosophers: Ehret, "Common Leadership Strategies ..."

48 Authentic people instil a sense of trust and earn respect: Berkeley Executive Education, "The Importance of Authenticity."

49 Living authentically leads to enhanced happiness: Wood et al., "The Authentic Personality," p.385.

50 90 percent of consumers look for authenticity from brands: DeGruttola, "Survey Reveals How Consumers Really Judge Brand Authenticity."

51 Authentic relationships lead to higher interpersonal trust: Wickham, "Perceived Authenticity in Romantic Partners."

52 Reflection from Michael Bungay Stanier in an email newsletter entitled "Can You Turn on Authentic?"

53 Western culture values boldness, while Asian cultures revere quiet and sensitivity: Cain, *Quiet,* p.189.

54 The most effective leadership changes from situation to situation: McAlpine, "Make Like a Chameleon."

55 'She'd probably prepared more than everyone else…': Cain, *Quiet,* p.8.

56 Quoted in Attar, *Debunking the Myths of Colonization: The Arabs and Europe,* p.9.

57 Churchill quote from 1906: Duranti, *The Conservative Human Rights Revolution*, p.125.

58 Churchill quoted on opposing women's right to vote: Langworth, "Churchill, Women's Suffrage ..." 2018.

59 The unreliable metric of GDP: Pilling, *The Growth Delusion*, p.10.

60 Richard Branson, Mark Zuckerberg, and Barack Obama have minimalist closets: Elkins, "Richard Branson ..."

61 Humans have mental frameworks or schemas for how to behave: Ripley, *High Conflict*.

62 We are often forced to see the world in just two dimensions: Ibid.

63 Oversimplification is happening in our thinking: Myers, "Why Oversimplification is Bad ..."

64 Using the internet is training our brains to be distracted: Carr, *The Shallows*, p.194.

65 Taking each other as individuals means we can react with thoughtfulness: Blake, "How Oversimplifying a Complex World Drives Us Apart."

66 Oversimplification is a recurring problem that takes us away from truth: Firestone, "Oversimplification in Philosophy," p.396.

67 New Zealand's creation of a wellbeing budget: Anderson and Mossialos, "Beyond Gross Domestic Product ...", p.320.

68 Moving past the GDP as the measure of society's progress: Hoekstra, *This is the Moment ...*

69 Cleverness is a sharp-focus lens, and wisdom a wide-angle lens: De Bono, *Teach Your Child How to Think*.

70 100 percent of conversational partners reached consensus after framing the debate as a problem with shades of gray: Grant, *Think Again*, p.164.

71 Presenting issues as complex does not undermine reader's trust: Van der Bles, *The Effects of Communicating Uncertainty*, p.7672.

72 Expressing doubt increases persuasiveness: Karmarker and Tormala, "Believe Me …", p.1033.

73 'A dose of complexity can upset certain cycles': Grant, *Think Again*, p.165.

74 High-reactive infants use more eye movements when making decisions: Cain, *Quiet*, p.103.

75 Going deep means you will also notice more: Davis, *Dedicated.*

76 Ibid., p.161.

77 "We can favour content and sources that present many sides": Grant, *Think Again,* p.161.

78 Taking each other as individuals means we can react with thoughtfulness: Blake, "How Oversimplifying a Complex World Drives Us Apart."

79 Asking questions that don't have a single answer: Grant, *Think Again*, p.189.

80 'The students become accustomed to asking …': Lipman, "About P4C."

81 Andre Gidé's quote on discovering new lands found in: Sincero, *You Are a Badass*, p.34.

82 'When you set out to tell a complex story, your narrative expands outward': Davis, *Dedicated,* p.154

83 When we take notes, 'we are forced to discriminate': Paul, *The Extended Mind*, p.152

84 "Often it is literally on the page that we do the work": Paul, ibid., p.152.

85 TED talks are no more than 18 minutes: Agarwal, "Why Are TED Talks 18 Minutes Long?"

86 1,300–2,000 characters are recommended for LinkedIn posts: Servar, "How Long Should a LinkedIn Post or Message Be?"

87 'Never mistake simplicity for elegance': Myers, "Why Oversimplification..."

88 'When people speak with certainty, we're more likely to think they are right': Berger, *Magic Words*, p.51.

89 European researchers brought together start-up founders: Camuffo et al., "A Scientific Approach ...".

90 Study on contentious topics: Hagmann & Loewenstein, "Persuasion with Motivated Beliefs."

91 It's physiologically normal to feel stress when we face the unknown: Zucker and Rowell, "6 Strategies for Leading Through Uncertainty."

92 The more we engage with a topic …": Bogart, *Raising Critical Thinkers*, p.136.

93 'You can be confident in your abilities …': Grant, *Think Again*, p.46.

94 'When competent individuals …': Chamorro-Premuzic, *Why Do So Many Incompetent Men Become Leaders?*, p.28.

95 'Wisdom arises from understanding the limitations': Kashdan, *The Art of Insubordination*, p.152.

96 Scientific discovery is akin to feeling around in dark rooms: Holmes, "The Case for Teaching Ignorance."

97 Scientific facts are solid or immutable: Paul, *The Extended Mind*.

98 Scientists are, ideally, curious, humble, and willing to test a hypothesis: Edmondson, *Right Kind of Wrong*.

99 Quote from Ed Catmull, as found in: Godin, *The Song of Significance*, p.82.

100 Teaching people about discoveries is not enough: Firestein, *Ignorance*.

101 'Remember you're supposed to update your belief ...': Kashdan, *The Art of Insubordination*, p.153.

102 'People tend to think of not knowing ...': Firestein, *Ignorance*, p.18.

103 We physically mirror other people's body language: Endedijk et al., "Neural Mirroring ..."

104 'An informed audience ...': Grant, *Think Again*, p.129.

105 Rufus Griscom's quote, as found in: Grant, *Originals*, p.73.

106 Story of Carl Weiman, as found in: Paul, *The Extended Mind*, p.188.

107 Ibid., p.189.

108 We did not evolve to solve tricky puzzles on our own: Mercier, *The Enigma of Reason.*

109 Ibid.

110 Being creative together far exceeds solo efforts: Gaston, *Find Your Sparkle.*

111 Consultation improved decision-making: Chia, "6 Management Styles: Advantages and Disadvantages."

112 Individuals feel less need to defend their ideas if others offer up alternatives: Ripley, *High Conflict.*

113 'The sage-on-the-stage ...': Grant, *Think Again*, p.192.

114 The command-and-control approach was discussed in a LinkedIn article from Bob Marcus on February 18, 2020.

115 The call for more democratic styles was discussed in a LinkedIn article from Mustahsan Ali on January 4, 2020.

116 There is a huge up-tick in crowdsourcing: Tucker, "How Crowdsourcing Can Enhance Innovation Performance."

117 A consultative approach gives students more agency: Jones, "A Guide to the Sidelines."

118 Learning with active engagement promotes understanding: Chaffee, "Nature Agrees."

119 'We invite them to join us as a partner': Grant, *Think Again*, p.129.

120 'The more people depend ...': Carr, *The Shallows*, p.216.

121 'There is an inherent limit for each of us ...': Zucker & Rowell. "6 Strategies for Leading Through Uncertainty."

122 People like feeling smart: Berger, *Magic Words*, p.75.

123 Ibid.

124 'The effort to try to feel happy is often precisely the thing that makes us miserable': Burkeman, *The Antidote*, p.7.

125 'If we approach an argument as war ...': Grant, *Think Again*, p.129.

126 Conflict seizes our attention: Paul, *The Extended Mind*.

127 We increase mental efforts to understand what's being communicated: Hoeks et al., "Questions Left Unanswered."

128 McKeown admits to cracks in the assumption that he could achieve everything. McKeown, *Effortless*, p.9.

129 'I was doing the right things for the wrong reasons ...' McKeown, *Effortless*, p.12.

130 'Writing this book ...': Curran, *The Perfection Trap*, p.10.

131 We are more likely to change our minds when we can do so privately: John et al., "The Self-Presentational Consequences.".

132 Suzi McAlpine's reference to research: Jeong et al., "Research: Changing Your Mind Makes You Seem Intelligent."

133 Concept of confident humility: Grant, *Think Again*.

134 The ability to change our minds helps us form better answers: Grant, *Think Again*.

135 Ibid., p.3.

136 Piaget discussed his cognitive theory in depth in *The Construction of Reality in the Child*. This source provides an accessible explanation: Main, "Assimilation Vs Accommodation."

137 'New ideas and observations are far from perfect on their day of birth …': Comstock, *Imagine it Forward*, p.231.

138 'Life rewards action, not intelligence': LinkedIn article from James Clear, 2023.

139 Clear reflects on his discussion with Richard Branson in: Clear, "Successful People."

140 Adam Grant's speaking fees: SpeakersU, "Best Business Speakers of 2023."

141 'I didn't have time to dip my toe …': Grant, *Hidden Potential*, p.54.

142 We often have ideas that we dismiss due to timing: Boyes, "5 Mistakes We Make ..."

143 'If I'd waited to know who I was …": Kleon, *Steal Like an Artist*, 27.

144 'Each one has been possible …': Kempton, *The Way of the Fearless Writer*, 164.

145 "A sign of doing challenging work …": Clear, "Successful People Start Before They're Ready."

146 "When we put questions out into the world …": Kempton, *The Way of the Fearless Writer*, 76.

147 Ibid., 139.

148 Real change takes time, such as gathering tinder for a fire: Davis, *Dedicated*.

149 Grant & Gladwell discussed the book in a TED podcast: "Unlocking Hidden Potential".

Christina Wedgwood

Christina has been helping to unlock better thinking, better content and better impact for her clients as a writer, coach and consultant since 2011.

Christina has always been led by the belief that ideas, words and stories have the power to influence the world towards better—and that thought leadership is a vital vehicle for transforming passion and purpose into something even more powerful.

As the founder and director of Intelligent Ink, Aotearoa New Zealand's first agency devoted to the practice of thought leadership, Christina has supported some of the largest brands, nonprofits, and solopreneurs in New Zealand and abroad. Today, Intelligent Ink focuses on empowering impact-driven experts to improve and evolve their thinking and leverage their ideas to lead us all towards something better. While she has helped transform dozens of thought leaders into published authors over the years, *Better* is the first book of her own.

Christina lives in Auckland with her husband and three young boys.

Made in United States
North Haven, CT
23 May 2025

69084693R00163